HOMOTOPIA?

BEFORE YOU START TO READ THIS BOOK, take this moment to think about making a donation to punctum books, an independent non-profit press,

@ http://punctumbooks.com/checkout/

If you're reading the e-book, you can click on the image below to go directly to our donations site. Any amount, no matter the size, is appreciated and will help us to keep our ship of fools afloat. Contributions from dedicated readers will also help us to keep our commons open and to cultivate new work that can't find a welcoming port elsewhere. Our adventure is not possible without your support.
Vive la open-access.

Fig. 1. Hieronymus Bosch, *Ship of Fools* (1490–1500)

Homotopia?: Gay Identity, Sameness and the Politics of Desire
© 2015 Jonathan Kemp

http://creativecommons.org/licenses/by-nc-sa/4.0/

This work carries a Creative Commons BY-NC-SA 4.0 International license, which means that you are free to copy and redistribute the material in any medium or format, and you may also remix, transform and build upon the material, as long as you clearly attribute the work to the authors (but not in a way that suggests the authors or punctum endorses you and your work), you do not use this work for commercial gain in any form whatsoever, and that for any remixing and transformation, you distribute your rebuild under the same license.

This work was originally written for a Master of Philosophy degree at Sussex University in 1997. Many thanks to Jonathan Dollimore for his supervision. A version of chapter 4 appeared as 'A Problem in Gay Heroics: John Addington Symonds and *l'amour de l'impossible*' (article/chapter) in *John Addington Symonds: Culture and the Demon Desire*, ed. John Pemble (Macmillan, 2000).

First published in 2015 by
punctum books
Brooklyn, New York
http://punctumbooks.com
ISBN-13: 978-0692606247
ISBN-10: 0692606246

Library of Congress Cataloging Data is available from the Library of Congress

Cover image: Matthew Stradling, "Tough Love"
Cover design: Eileen Joy
Typographic design: Vincent W.J. van Gerven Oei

Jonathan Kemp

homotopia?

*Gay Identity,
Sameness and the
Politics of Desire*

punctum books
2015

Contents

INTRODUCTION
Refusals | 9

CHAPTER ONE
Against Custom:
André Gide's Pedagogic Pederasty | 31

CHAPTER TWO
No Such Things as Homosexuals:
Marcel Proust and 'La race maudite' | 53

CHAPTER THREE
Beautiful Flowers and Perverse Ruins:
Edward Carpenter's Intermediate Sex | 75

CHAPTER FOUR
A Problem in Gay Heroics:
John Addington Symonds and l'amour de l'impossible | 99

CONCLUSION
Fear of a Gay Anus | 121

BIBLIOGRAPHY | 137

Introduction

Refusals

> "There is not one corner of the earth where the alleged
> crime of sodomy has not had shrines and votaries."
> – Marquis de Sade, *Philosophy in the Bedroom*

> "Maybe the target nowadays is not to discover what we are,
> but to refuse what we are [...]. We have to promote new forms of
> subjectivity through the refusal of this kind of individuality."
> – Michel Foucault, 'The Subject and Power'

Do opposites attract? *Is* desire lack? These assumptions have become so much a part of the ways in which we conceive desire that they are rarely questioned. Yet, what do they say about how homosexuality – a desire for the same – is viewed in our culture? This book takes as its starting point the absence of a suitable theory of homosexual desire, a theory not predicated on such heterological assumptions.[1] It is an investigation into how such assumptions acquired meaning within homosexual discourse, and as such is offered as an interruption within the hegemony of desire, a withdrawal of allegiance "from the old categories of the Negative (law, limit, castration, lack, lacuna) which Western thought has so long held sacred as a form of power and an ac-

---

[1] By 'heterological' I mean a logic based on difference rather than sameness. The assumption that all desire can be reduced to lack is heterological. See Georges Bataille, 'The Use Value of D.A.F. de Sade', in *Visions of Excess: Selected Writings 1927–1939*, trans. A. Stoeckl, University of Minnesota Press, 1985, 91–102, where he writes about the "heterological theory of knowledge" (97).

cess to reality".[2] As such, homosexual desire constitutes the biggest challenge to Western binaric thinking in that it dissolves the sacred distinctions between Same/Other, Desire/Identification, subject/object, male/female.

Under the epistemological regime of Lack/Difference,[3] homosexual desire has become heterosexualised, and a hierarchical binarism of penetrator/penetrated is established within which the egality of a same-sex pairing is ignored. Without equality of status for both the anus and the phallus, there can be no true or complete sense of homosexual desire.

The book investigates the development of a homosexual discourse at the end of the nineteenth century and the beginning of the twentieth century, and examines how that discourse worked with heterosexualized models of desire. The texts discussed were published between the years 1891 and 1924, an historical moment when the concept of a distinct homosexual 'identity' took shape within a medicalized discourse centred on essential identity traits and characteristics. Prior to the medicalization of 'the homosexual', sex between men was regarded as a sin to which all men were vulnerable; after around 1870, it became the expression of a distinct and innate nature. The four primary texts to be discussed all work within this rubric of science, contributing to a discourse which saw the human race divided into two distinct categories: heterosexuals and homosexuals. How did this division come about, and what were its effects? How was this discourse sustained, and how were the meanings it produced received? For men whose erotic interest was exclusively in other men, what did it mean to see oneself and one's desires as the outcome of biology rather than moral lapse?

Etymologically, 'homosexuality' means a desire for the same (*homos* = Greek for 'same'), rather than the usual androcentric interpretation of a desire for men (*homo* = Latin for 'man');

---

2 Michel Foucault, Preface to Deleuze, G. & F. Guattari, *Anti-Oedipus: Capitalism and Schizophrenia* [1972], trans. R. Hurley et al., University of Minnesota Press, 1983.

3 This regime works primarily within a psychoanalytic framework, based on the work of Freud and Lacan. See J. Rose and J. Mitchell, *Feminine Sexuality: Jacques Lacan and the Ecole Freudienne*, Macmillan, 1982; K. Lewes, *The Psychoanalytic Theory of Male Homosexuality*, Quartet, 1989.

an interpretation with which lesbians have been understandably uncomfortable.[4] In a culture which champions so-called 'masculine traits' and misogynistically undervalues so-called 'feminine traits', the discursive and physical violence against the effeminate man is more consistent than that against the butch lesbian. Consider that a word was invented – effeminate – specifically to designate a man who acts womanly, but no word has been invented to describe exclusively a woman acting manly.[5] Could this be because it is perfectly understandable within a heterosexual patriarchy that a woman would aspire to be a man (what Freud called 'penis envy'), and utterly inconceivable that a man might aspire to be a woman, might want to abdicate his precious male privilege (no theory on 'vagina envy')? This thesis argues that for a man to desire men does not equate with aspiring to be a woman.

Andre Gide's *Corydon*, Edward Carpenter's *The Intermediate Sex*, and John Addington Symond's *A Problem in Modern Ethics* are all pseudo-scientific texts written by non-medical men of letters, and were, in their time, highly influential on the emerging homosexual discourse. The fourth text I will examine, the twenty-odd pages of Marcel Proust's novel *A la recherche de temps perdu* usually referred to as 'La race maudite', is the most problematic, in that it appeared under the guise of fiction. Its inclusion here is based on evidence that Proust originally planned this 'essay-within-a-novel' to be published separately. In it, he offers a pseudo-scientific theory of male–male love. It is as a piece of non-fiction that I shall approach this segment of Proust's novel.

---

[4] Within medical discourse, lesbianism was seen as resulting from a male soul trapped in a woman's body, the exact converse of the male model. In this way, lesbian intercourse was heterosexualized along identical lines, with the top being stereotypically masculine (butch), the bottom stereotypically 'femme'. There are no examples, however, of lesbian writers responding in a similar way to this medical model until Radclyffe Hall's *The Well of Loneliness* in 1928. A lesbian 'reverse discourse' did not emerge until the *Well of Loneliness* trials. See Jonathan Dollimore, *Sexual Dissidence: Augustine to Wilde, Freud to Foucault*, Oxford University Press, 1991, 48–52; 62.

[5] "Consider how the two semantically opposed, morphologically identical words, effeminate and emasculate [...], instead of together defining a state of genderlessness, synonymously converge in a single attribute that may be predicated only of men." D.A. Miller, *Bringing Out Roland Barthes*, University of California Press, 1992, 15.

What all four texts reveal is an extreme level of anxiety around sex, especially anal intercourse. Why did these texts deny, ignore or minimize anal sex?[6] Why did they accept and therefore maintain the medical stereotype of the passive sodomite, rather than energize a radical departure from the conflation of homosexuality with gender inversion? Moreover, have they done homosexuality a huge disservice by accepting and perpetuating the link between same-sex desire and medicine (not to mention between same-sex desire and effeminacy)? How far has this belief in the inferiority of the 'passive' partner informed our modern concepts of gay identity, to the extent that some tops believe themselves to be in some way more male than (i.e., better than) the men they fuck? Could it be that some tops rely on this mimesis of heterosexual positioning in order to feel less of a homosexual (and therefore minimizing the inferior status allotted them within a homophobic culture)? Does this assumption that sexual passivity = effeminacy (and vice versa) determine gay men's choices of sexual partner and sexual act, as well as affecting their self-image and self-esteem? (One need only look at the personal ads in the gay press to see how phobically this stereotype has been installed: 'non-FM', or 'no effems' invariably appears alongside 'straight-acting').

These four texts supply clues to how this discourse came to acquire meaning; how it shaped the perception of homosexuality as the expression of a particular type of person, rather than a sexual behaviour available to anybody. In this way, hegemonic notions of gender – the dominant social meanings of the categories *man* and *woman* – were increasingly seen as teleological.

Proust, Gide, Carpenter and Symonds were all fiction writers or poets. They were also homosexuals. As such, their pseudo-scientific responses to the medical colonization[7] of their desires

---

6   Given the historical evidence for the practice of sodomy in the period before and the period after that in which these writers worked, one must assume that anal sex didn't suddenly take a drop in popularity.

7   See Colin Spencer, *Homosexuality: A History*, Fourth Estate, 1995, Chapter 11: 'Colonisation by Medicine'. The concept of colonization in connection with the medicalisation of homosexuality is particularly apposite given this book's preoccupation with 'reverse discourse', for colonization was as much to do with language as with anything else. Fou-

dramatizes Foucault's theory of reverse discourse. These four men wrote from a position of subjectivity, of first hand experience, acceding to the scientific nomination and yet resisting the objective naming from elsewhere, from outside, naming themselves. In this sense, their work is important in establishing a foundation for a discourse on identity politics which came to the fore in the last twentieth century and which has more recently been the subject of great scrutiny.[8] The 'authority' of medicine gave these writers the opportunity, and permission, to write about what had hitherto been hidden or shrouded in normative discourse. It also gave them the opportunity to adopt the freshly polished category of 'the homosexual' and invigorate it with a liberationist politics.[9]

These four writers were also, to greater or lesser degrees, homosexual pioneers, gay icons, seen as breaking new ground, making radical claims, and paving the way for our contemporary discourse on homosexual politics, their work rallying points for a nascent community and affirmative voices in the dark for isolated individuals in need of a life-line. They are our forefathers. There is, however, a certain nostalgia implicit in this way of seeing them which complicates their value and often forecloses proper critique. Late 60s–early 70s Gay Liberation, for example, unearthed the writings of Edward Carpenter and saw in them an historical precursor of coming out.[10]

---

cault speaks of the homosexual using the same language as the one which constitutes the medical discourse by which he is disqualified, in a scenario analogous to the way in which non-whites had to master the tongue of the colonials in order to articulate dissent.

8 See, for example, Judith Butler, *Gender Trouble: Feminism and the Subversion of Identity*, Routledge, 1990.

9 There were other literary men who took up the pen as doctors: the poet Marc Raffalovich, *Uranisme et unisexualité* (1896); Xavier Mayne [Edward Irenaeus Prime Stevenson], *The Intersexes: Simisexualism as a Problem in Modern Life* (1908). There were also men of science, such as Havelock Ellis and Sigmund Freud, who wrote on literature.

10 See, for example, Noel Grieg's Introduction to Edward Carpenter's *Selected Writings*, vol. 1: *Sex*, Gay Men's Press, 1984: "A century before homosexuals stepped out of the closets en masse, to add our voices to the demands for great changes amongst the masses, Edward Carpenter took that route as an individual" (38); Jeffrey Weeks, *Coming Out: Homosexual Politics in Britain from the Nineteenth Century to the Present*, Quartet, 1977, pp.68–83; Weeks and Rowbotham, *Socialism and the New Life: The Personal and Sexual Politics of Edward Carpenter and Havelock Ellis*, Pluto Press, 1997. Ian Young, in *The*

Today, Carpenter and Symonds are largely forgotten, Gide outmoded, Proust rarely read, yet they nevertheless played an important role in the formation of a homosexual discourse. So whilst it is vitally important to critique them and not consider them beyond reproach, it is still as important to attempt to empathise with their position and to credit them for opening up debates which had been tighty shut, and making possible the current discourse from which a critique such as this book can be made. To use Carpenter again, his writings on male–male love appeared in the aftermath of the Wilde trials; when the realistic and popular thing to do was keep your mouth shut, he continued to publish essays on 'homogenic love'. We might disagree now with what he wrote, but we cannot deny his bravery.

It is debatable whether these writers could have done otherwise but adopt the heterological medical model, given the theoretical tools available to them. Foucault, whilst being highly critical of liberationist discourse, nonetheless recognized the necessity of this discursive reversal of the medical model in the constitution of alternative sexual lifestyles. By taking the medical model literally, and thereby turning it around, these writers were, in effect, saying, "All right, we are what you say we are – by nature, disease, or perversion, as you like. Well, if that's what we are, let's be it, and if you want to know what we are, we can tell you ourselves better than you can."[11] As Foucault states, "It is the strategic turnabout of one and the 'same' will to truth."[12] These documents contributed to the construction of that 'truth'. Through being homosexuals themselves, these writers were not merely commenting on the topic of homosexuality, they were preparing the ground for a stylistics of existence, creating an ethics of homosexuality, and defining the methodology of gay identity politics. For this reason, the texts are discussed in reverse chronology, as a way of moving towards the beginnings of this homosexual discourse, of stripping it down, working back

---

Stonewall Experiment, Cassell, 1995, goes as far as to call him 'Ted', the name by which he was known to friends (30).

11 Michel Foucault, quoted in David Halperin, *Saint Foucault: Towards a Gay Hagiography*, Oxford University Press, 1995, 58.

12 Ibid., 59.

through its history to reveal its origins, to reveal that it could not have been other than it was. It is, in the Foucauldian sense, an archeology, asking "How is it that one particular statement appeared rather than another? [...] what is this specific existence that emerges from what is said and nowhere else?"[13] How did the 'truth' of homosexuality acquire meaning, and what are its limits, its exclusions? How do these four texts, these four statements, connect, and how do they differ in the construction of that 'truth'? And, ultimately, is that 'truth' still true one hundred years on?

Discursive Reversal

The book takes as axiomatic Foucault's claim that a reverse discourse emerged in response to the medical 'invention' of the homosexual in the late nineteenth century. This reverse discourse was a fluke response exceeding the discursive requirements of the medical discourse which sought merely to categorise and proscribe sexual behaviours and types as a way of establishing a surveillance of the body and thus broadening the field of social control. However, as Foucault writes:

> It also make possible the formation of a 'reverse' discourse: homosexuality began to speak in its own behalf, to demand that its legitimacy or 'naturality' be acknowledge, often in the same vocabulary, using the same categories by which it was medically disqualified.[14]

This reverse discourse would seem to be

> a mixture both of something more and of something less than a simple negation. On the one hand, a repetition amounting to acceptance of homosexuality as a personal identity; and,

---

[13] Michel Foucault, *The Archeology of Knowledge*, trans. A.M. Sheridan Smith, Harper Colophon, 1976.
[14] Michel Foucault, *The History of Sexuality*, vol. 1: *An Introduction*, Penguin, 1979, 101. Subsequent references will appear in the body of the text, parenthesized and indicated by the abbreviation HS.

on the other hand, an appropriation consisting in turning to advantage this imposed identity.[15]

It is a subjectivation that exceeds the normalizing aims by which it is mobilized. At the same time as constituting a form of resistance to power, this reverse discourse was also a strategy of power itself, for, as Foucault tells us, "there is not, on the one side, a discourse of power, and opposite it another discourse that runs counter to it", but, rather, "discourses are tactical elements or blocks operating in the field of force relations; there can exist different and even contradictory discourses within the same strategy" (HS, 101–2). The very tools of domination are used as the tools of resistance; the homosexual subject embraces his new subjectivity and proceeds to vocalize his experiences in the new language available. As Judith Butler writes, "sometimes the very term that would annihilate us becomes the site of resistance, the possibility of an enabling social and political signification".[16]

Foucault's theory of discourse is a positive power-model, allowing for conflictual movements. The category of 'homosexual' was not simply imposed from above on passive subjects; the efficacy was undermined by the homosexuals' response as much as it was aided by their willingness to be defined in medical terms. It was a contradictory discourse, a strategic move "designed to justify claims for homosexual rights".[17] It took the form of political resistance. And these four texts bear witness to the political struggle for the right to define oneself, as much as they represent the ways in which the medical model was employed within the emergent identity politics of this discourse.

The most strategic approach to legislative reform became a capitulation to the medical model, because if homosexuals could be seen as having been 'born that way' and therefore constituting a recognizable minority (a 'third sex'), then they

---
15 Diane Macdonell, *Theories of Discourse: An Introduction*, Basil Blackwell, 1986, 117.
16 Judith Butler, 'Critically Queer' in GLQA: *A Journal of Lesbian & Gay Studies*, 1.1 (1993), 22.
17 Alan Sinfield, *The Wilde Century: Effeminacy, Oscar Wilde and the Queer Moment*, Cassell, 1994, 14.

deserved tolerance and legal equality.[18] As such, this reverse discourse, working within the same field of force relations as the discourse which identified homosexuality as a distinct category, wielded enormous power; in this case, the power to legitimate the scientific claim for the great 'homo/hetero divide.'[19] By accepting the new category 'homosexual' – for however radical a purpose – homosexuals consigned themselves to a 'third sex', recognizable by the diacritical marker of effeminacy.

This acceptance of a distinct category also hypostasized and reified 'heterosexuality', securing a binaric divide of not only gender but also sexual orientation. Further – and of greater concern for this book – if, as Foucault seems to suggest, this response to a medical categorization was the foundation of an emerging 'gay identity' to which we are heirs – what consequences did the denial of anal sex by these writers have on that emergent identity? How far can we see their apparent acceptance of the stereotype of the kind of homosexual who enjoyed anal sex as actually *thwarting* that identity? Could it be that the concept of gay identity inherited from this reverse discourse has imported more or less wholesale the medical model of active = male/passive = female to such an extent that "most gays feel the passive role is in some way demeaning"[20]? Did these responses to the medical discourse unwittingly saddle future generations of homosexuals with a conceptual model of desire

---

18 A similar reasoning fuels the gay gene or brain argument. Simon Le Vay, the chief proponent of this, himself a gay neurologist, argues for recognition within the American Constitution for legal equality, based on the fact that, genetically, homosexuality constitutes a similar status to race or gender. See Le Vay, *The Sexual Brain*, MIT Press, 1994.

19 David Halperin writes that this division of the human race into two distinct groups of people, "who possess two distinct kinds of subjectivity, who are inwardly oriented in a specific direction, and who therefore belong to separate and determinate human species", does not "represent merely new ways of classifying persons – that is, innovations in moral and judicial language – but new types of desire, new kinds of desiring human beings" (*One Hundred Years of Homosexuality*, Routledge, 1990, 43). Eve Kosofsky Sedgwick claims that the homo/heterosexual definition is responsible for the crisis that has fractured "many of the major nodes of thought and knowledge in twentieth century Western culture." Her *Epistemology of the Closet* (University of California Press, 1993) argues "that an understanding of virtually any aspect of modern Western culture must be, not merely incomplete, but damaged in its central substance to the degree that it does not incorporate a critical analysis of modern homo/heterosexual definition" (1).

20 Michel Foucault, *Foucault Live (Interviews 1966–84)*, Semiotext(e), 1989, 277.

that is no more than an alarmingly inaccurate mimesis of the heterosexual coupling, a conceptual model that rapidly became a concrete and resilient stereotype?

The horror surrounding what Foucault calls "that utterly confused category" (HS, 101): sodomy, would seem to stem from its non-procreative use, and as such, there was no distinction necessary within ancient canonical law between the various types of sodomy: male–male, male–female, or human–animal. However, increasing use of sodomy as a definitional term for male–male desire throughout history, culminating in the translation of 'the sodomite' into 'the homosexual', bears witness to the conflation of the act with a specific sexual orientation. Furthermore, as the 1986 Bowers vs. Hardwick case in the States has shown,[21] there is now a clear distinction drawn within the law between heterosexual and homosexual sodomy, the latter punishable by law, the former invisible and/or acceptable.

Lee Edelman suggests that men "must repudiate the pleasures of the anus because their fulfillment allegedly presupposes, and inflicts, the loss or 'wound' that serves as the very definition of femaleness".[22] The prohibition against anal sex between men goes to work even before the actual fulfillment of anal pleasure, on the very thought itself. In his history of British criminal law, Sir Leon Radzinowicz refers to the unnameable nature of sodomy, the impossibility of giving it a name, "lest its very definition inflict a lasting wound on the morals of the people."[23] Could this be what Symonds means when he calls homosexuality 'the love of the impossible'? Not only the impossibility of love between men but also the impossibility of expressing that love physically without cultural erasure, cultural castration. Given recent work on queer performativity by Butler and Sedgwick,[24] one can read

---

[21] See 'Bowers vs Harwick' in Jonathan Goldberg, *Reclaiming Sodom*, Routledge, 1994, 117–42; see also Janet E. Halley, 'The Politics of the Closet: Towards Equal Protection for Gay, Lesbian and Bisexual Identity', in ibid., 145–90; Lee Edelman, *Homographesis*, Routledge, 1994, 129–137; and Sedgwick, *Epistemology of the Closet*, 74–82.

[22] Lee Edelman, 'Seeing Things: Representation, the Scene of Surveillance and the Spectacle of Gay Male Sex', in D. Fuss (ed.), *Inside/Out*, Routledge, 1991, 106.

[23] Quoted in Edelman, *Homographesis*, 5.

[24] Judith Butler, *Excitable Speech: A Politics of the Performative*, Routledge, 1997, and 'Critically Queer', in GLQA 1.1, 1993; Eve Sedgwick, 'Queer Performativity: Henry James' The

this unnameability of anal sex between men as a linguistic omission of the act itself. To name it is not only to inflict a so-called moral wound but also to give it a reality that might encourage further replication of the act itself; saying it becomes as good (or bad) as doing it. Indeed, saying it is doing it. Sodomy, in this sense, is a performative, is 'the love that dare not speak its name'.

In real, physical terms, of course, to be penetrated by another man does not result in castration. The phallic loss is a cultural prohibition on a behaviour deemed dangerous to the sexual status quo; the maintenance of the Law of the Phallus is only possible through the avoidance of this psychic loss. A 'real' man does not get buggered; therefore, to get buggered must cost one one's masculinity; one abdicates one's phallic privilege. In this exchange, the anus becomes the wound which defines one as female. The punishment, therefore, in a gynaecophobic culture, is cultural castration. The so-called passive partner must pay for his pleasure by being seen – and seeing himself – as somehow less than a man. Given that, in cultural terms, all homosexuals are construed as 'passive' (i.e., not truly active like real – straight – men), and given also that ours is a culture "always predisposed to observe and condemn the proffered 'ass' in 'passive'",[25] this has resulted in a widespread and ongoing programme whose sole aim is the insistence on the essential and ineradicable femininity of all homosexuals; a femininity which finds its fulfillment in an almost pathological anal passivity.

So, whilst the reverse discourse exemplified in the writings examined here allowed for the development of a specifically gay identity and for cultural representation within the register of minority status, it was only able to do so within a scientifically validated 'feminine paradigm' which claimed the homosexual as a race apart, a third sex; a 'woman's soul trapped in a man's body'.

This project is concerned not simply with the more or less exclusive cultural association of anal sex with male homosexuality, but, more importantly, its association with a particular type

---

Art of the Novel', in ibid.
25 Edelman, *Homographesis*, 24.

of homosexuality: namely, effeminacy. As such, it constitutes a vindication for the right of – in porn-speak – the Butch Bottom. Drawing from the theoretical work of Guy Hocquenghem, Mario Miele, and, more recently, Leo Bersani, I will conclude with a rehearsal of an anal politics, a reclamation of the anus as a pleasure zone, a sexual organ in its own right, without reference to the normative tropes of gender or gender inversion.

The Dominant Fiction

Rancière's term 'dominant fiction', as well as suggesting the artifice of ideology, usefully confuses the literary and the scientific, the two categories with which this study is concerned. The fact that it was novelists and poets who took up the gauntlet thrown down by the medical categorization of the homosexual suggests that reverse discourse is an act not only of immense bravery but also of great imagination. Resistence is not just a negation, but an act of creation. So it seems apposite that it should be poets and novelists who responded. Indeed, the man who invented the word 'homosexual' wasn't a doctor, as is usually assumed, but a novelist, Karl Maria Kertbeny (1824–1882).[26] Under the pseudonym Benkert, he published two pamphlets in which he called for full legal rights for homosexuals. In this struggle, he shared a goal with Karl Heinrich Ulrichs (1825–1895), a jurist whose own series of liberationist pseudo-scientific pamphlets appeared between 1862–1874, in which he outlined his theory of *anima muliebris in corpore virili inclusa,* or 'a woman's soul trapped in a man's body.'[27] The two men corresponded for a while but differed greatly on their understanding of male–male love.

According to Ulrichs, the human embryo contained two important 'germs': one which would develop into the psyche or soul, and another which would become the body. In most people there was a synchronicity between the two germs, i.e., both

---

26 See Frederic Silverstolpe, 'Benkert Was Not a Doctor: On the Nonmedical Origins of the Homosexual Category in the Nineteenth Century', unpublished conference paper, 1987; and Hubert Kennedy, *Ulrichs: The Life and Times of Karl Heinrich Ulrichs, Pioneer of the Modern Gay Movement,* Alyson Publications, 1988, 149–56.

27 For a detailed account of Ulrichs' life and work, see Kennedy, *Ulrichs.*

were of the same sex (resulting in heterosexual desire). Therefore, Ulrichs argued, in the case of homosexuals, "nature developed the male germ [...] physically but the female spiritually",[28] resulting in Urnings, or physically 'normal' men who, possessing a female spirit, desire other men. The object of desire for such a being, however, would not be other Urnings, but virile, heterosexual men.

In the light of correspondence from other Urnings, Ulrichs' subsequent pamphlets expanded his theories to incorporate other types of Urnings, but this only succeeds in showing up the futility of such taxonomic thinking. For once one has set up 'the homosexual/Urning' as a separate species with a clearly identifiable set of characteristics and a morphology all its own, the potential for same-sex desire in those not conforming to such a prescriptive type is immediately foreclosed. Should one then attempt to accommodate diversity within one's theory, to allocate subspecies – as Ulrichs did with his *Weiblings* and *Mannlings* and *Uranodioninges* – surely one disqualifies one's entire premise that there is such a species; one would have to conclude that sexuality is manifold and malleable. The theory cannot withstand the weight of experiential data.

Like Symonds and Gide after him, Ulrichs sought to enhance the validity of his theories through association with a man of medicine. To this end he sent copies of his pamphlets to Richard von Krafft-Ebing, believing to have found in him an ally. Krafft-Ebing wrote to Ulrichs claiming that, "it was the knowledge of your writings alone that induced me to the study of this highly important field". But on publication of Krafft-Ebing's famous *Psychopathia Sexualis* in 1886, in which he describes homosexuals as suffering from a serious sexual pathology, Ulrichs regretted courting such support. After that, he referred to Krafft-Ebng as his "scientific opponent".[29]

Whereas Ulrichs' theory was predicated on a feminization of the male soul, Benkert asserted his masculinity and his aversion

---

28 Quoted in John Lauritsen and David Thorstad, *The Early Homosexual Rights Movement (1864–1935)*, Times Change Press, 1974, 47.
29 Kennedy, *Ulrichs*, 71.

to effeminate men. This possibly contributed to his coining the term, 'homosexual', a desire for the same sex, which he formulated alongside the concept of 'heterosexuality', a desire for the opposite sex. However, with an arbitrariness bordering on arrogance, late nineteenth century psychiatry adopted Benkert's word and attached it to Ulrichs' theory, and homosexuality was henceforth synonymous with gender inversion.

To realize that such a fundamental tenet of scientific thinking on male–male desire has such non-medical – even literary – origins (Ulrichs wrote poems and in 1885 published *Matrosengeschichten* [*Sailor Stories*], a collection of homo-erotic short stories; Benkert was a novelist); to acknowledge that Ulrichs' work was adopted widely and unproblematically by scientific writers such as Krafft-Ebing, Forel, Rohlet, Laurent and Westphal, is to call into question the very objectivity and exclusivity upon which the discipline of science is predicated. It suggests a lack of boundaries between the two disciplines, despite the fact that by the latter half of the nineteenth century science had begun to define itself as a pure and exclusive epistemological field into which not everyone could gain access; a field based on hard empiricism and objective research – a world of facts, in contrast to the flighty, airy, fantasy world of literature.

This more or less wholesale employment of Benkert's terms homosexual and heterosexual – as opposed to Ulrichs' urning and dioning, for example – is the clearest illustration of an isthmus connecting the literary and the medical. And it was this very porosity of the boundaries between science and literature that enabled Proust, Gide, Symonds and Carpenter to write pseudo-scientific texts. Moreover, this conflation of the two theories occurred at a time when a discursive visibility was afforded to same-sex desire through such public scandals as Boulton and Park and the Oscar Wilde trials, which foregrounded the cross-gender trope.[30]

Yet, why were Benkert's terms adopted over Ulrichs'? One reason is that the former weren't embedded in a complex sci-

---

30 See Neil Bartlett, *Who Was That Man? A Present For Mr. Oscar Wilde*, Serpent's Tail, 1989; Richard Ellman, *Oscar Wilde*, Hamish Hamilton, 1987.

entific theory and could therefore be taken up with reasonable ease; another is that homosexual/heterosexual sound more clinical, more scientific, than Ulrichs' overly poetic terms, and therefore served more readily the medical discourse's interest in objectifying or de-politicizing, the work of these emancipationists.

Benkert believed that regardless of whether homosexuality was inborn or not, what was needed was equality before the law. His writings were a tactical move, written from a radical position of defiance rather than Ulrichs' more apologetic position of a victim pleading leniency. Silverstolpe calls this the 'interest-model', "where the historical invention of the homosexual category consciously serves the purpose to promote the legal and social interests of homosexually interested people",[31] and contrasts it with the 'power-model' of later thinkers like Michel Foucault and Jeffrey Weeks who, in his view, see homosexuals as passive victims of a domineering medical discourse. Reverse discourse was an act of resistance, however, involving autonomy, agency, politicalisation and creativity – it is not simply a 'passive victim theory'.[32]

Silverstolpe argues that the medical intervention was a response to the liberationist categorization of the homosexual by the likes of Ulrichs and Benkert, "as well as an effort to control and redefine this new category when it was *already there*" (my emphasis). Therefore, the political move to reform the German penal code inspired the focus of medical attention, resulting in the unlikely marriage – what Silverstolpe calls an "unholy alliance" – of homosexual politics with normative science. Without this alliance, we might today conceptualize same-sex desire very differently.

However, rather than see it as an either/or, chicken-or-egg scenario, it may be more profitable to conceive the two discourses as emerging simultaneously, both feeding off and into each

---

31 Silverstolpe, 'Benkert Was Not a Doctor'.
32 This is a common criticism leveled at Foucault, who is seen by his critics as promoting a unidirectional, top–down concept of power; see Lois McNay, *Foucault: A Critical Introduction*, Polity Press, 1994, chapter 3 'From Discipline to Government'. Yet, Foucault explicitly states that power is multidirectional, with no primary or privileged site, and that "where there is power, there is resistence" (*HS*, 95).

other in a symbiotic relationshop that culminated in the dominance of the scientific discourse due to the imbalance of power and the disenfranchised, minority status of the homosexual subject. Above all, it was a question of politics. This unholy alliance was only possible because, initially, sexology was viewed, as Weeks[33] has pointed out, as a radical science, capable of altering the ways in which we thought about sex and sexuality. Why else would homosexuals like Ulrichs, Symonds, and Gide court allegiances with doctors?

But, emerging as it did within the normative sciences, sexology soon capitulated to societal and medical norms, casting the homosexual into the role of a diseased and degenerate being. Arguably, this could not have been otherwise, given that the majority of doctors were heterosexual and therefore approached the topic from their normative (and privileged) condition and construed in the homosexual act a mimesis of male–female intercourse. Much more surprising is the fact that these norms remained unchallenged in the work of these homosexual writers.

As Lauritsen and Thorstad point out, Ulrichs' ideas "left their mark upon several decades of ideology – especially in medical literature – and upon popular thinking".[34] Indeed, more than several decades later, in 1994, an article in The Independent quoted a neurologist who claims that gay men constitute, in neurological terms at least, a "third sex".[35] Like some phantom of the fin de siècle, biologism seems to be rearing its ugly head again, in the shape of a gay neurologist named Simon Le Vay, who states his allegiance with Ulrichs, believing the latter's ideas hold a "kernal of truth".[36]

---

33 Jeffrey Weeks, 'Questions of Identity', in *Against Nature: Essays on History, Sexuality and Identity*, Rivers Oram Press, 1981, 73; see also Wayne Koestenbaum, *Double Talk: The Erotics of Male Literary Collaboration*, Routledge, 1989, 43–7.
34 Lauritsen & Thorstad, *The Early Homosexual Rights Movement*, 47.
35 Sharon Kingman, 'Nature Not Nurture?', *The Independent on Sunday*, October 4, 1994.
36 Simon Le Vay, *The Sexual Brain*, MIT Press 1994, 109. Subsequent page references will appear in brackets in the main text, indicated by the abbreviation SB. Le Vay's research into the hypothalamus has led him to propose a neurological factor in sexual orientation, based on his findings that a particular section of the hypothalamus was larger in heterosexual men than in gay men, in whom it was the same size as in heterosexual woman (or at least Le Vay assumes his female brain sample came from straight women, though he has no way of knowing. His theoretical approach is highly suspect, based

Birke and Whisman have remarked on the dangers lurking within the biological model, as well as the dangers concomitant with its rejection. To reject the biological model is to side with the homophobes, who have changed tack and are now promoting homosexuality as a choice which should be avoided rather than a natural drive which cannot be altered.[37] And yet, to accept the biological model is surely to condone an essentialism that posits sexuality as immutable and innate, which doesn't move the debate any further on than it was a century ago.

In his use of quotations from Shakespeare for his chapter headings, Le Vay exemplifies the dialectical relationship between literature and science. Taking his cue from Ulrichs, Le Vay seems to think he has a poet's soul trapped in a neurologist's body: "Like waterlilies, we swing to and fro with the currents of life, yet our roots moor us each to our own spot on the river's floor" (SB, 138). What to make of this pseudo-poetic reflection in a work of science, a book whose aim is to focus "on the brain mechanisms that are responsible for sexual behaviour and feelings" (SB, xi)?

Le Vay's work perilously ignores the historical complexity and contingency involved in human sexuality, and its reductiveness should warn us against the adoption of biological explanations, which invariably work with a priori notions of gender and sexuality which frame and focus the research. Gender and sexu-

---

on assumptions about what constitutes 'normal' sex role behaviour, and riddled with shocking stereotypes about gay men. For example, he speculates on the atypicality of the gay male brain sample due to its having come from gay men who died from AIDS: "Are gay men who die of AIDS representative of gay men as a whole, or are they atypical, for example in preferring receptive anal intercourse (the major risk factor in homosexual sex) or in having unusually large numbers of sexual partners [...]?" (121). As Leo Bersani points out in 'Is the Rectum a Grave?', *October* 43 (1987), a certain gay male sexuality (anally receptive) has become associated with the worst cultural stereotypes of female sexuality: a nymphomaniac desire to be the receptacle for an endless stream of erections. For a detailed account of the 'gay gene' project, see Dean Hamer and Peter Copeland, *The Science of Desire: The Search For the Gay Gene and the Biology of Behaviour*, Simon & Schuster, 1994.

37 Lynda Birke, 'Zipping up the genes: Putting biological theories back in the closet', in *Perversions* 1 (Winter 1994), 38–50; Vera Whisman, *Queer By Choice: Lesbians, Gay Men and the Politics of Identity*, Routledge 1996, esp. 1–6. See also, Jennifer Terry, 'The Seductive Power of Science and the Making of Deviant Subjectivity', in Vernon A. Rosario, *Science and Homosexualities*, Routledge 1997, 271–89.

ality become associated with the 'right' genes in what amounts to a frighteningly eugenicist argument. In an approach reminiscent of early sexologists, homosexuality is literally written on the body, encoded indisputably in the hieroglyphics of our DNA. Once again, the homosexual body is marked by difference.

The Masculinist Model

"The third sex has been a powerful metaphor, virtually monopolizing the image of homosexuals in social life for the last one hundred years."[38] It has also, according to Gert Hekma, been a metaphor highly charged with shame, and as such has "prevented the development of gay identities" because those men unwilling to identify as a third sex/gender were unable to formulate a sense of self.

Yet there was an alternative to the effeminacy model – what we might call the masculinist model, centred around a small movement in Germany at the turn of the century, which refuted medical norms and claimed that homosexuality was an issue of culture and art rather than biology. Violently opposed to Hirschfeld and his third sex, the Community of Self-Owners (*Gemeinschaft der Eigenen*) promoted male bonding as the bedrock of culture, and sexual love between men as the pinnacle of masculinity.[39] But this model was not adopted and given wider application, as the third sex model was. Why?

A complex combination of factors contributed to the effeminacy model's sovereign rule:

1. *Economic*. Doctors and psychiatrists were keen to establish themselves as professionals and the cornering of the market offered by the effeminacy model provided them with a whole

---

38 Gert Hekma, "'A Female Soul in a Male Body": Sexual Inversion as Gender Inversion in Nineteenth Century Sexology', in G. Herdt (ed.), *Third Sex, Third Gender: Sexual Dimorphism in Culture and History*, Zone Books, 1994, 239.

39 See Harry Oosterhuis & Hubert Kennedy (eds), *Homosexuality and Male Bonding in Pre-Nazi Germany*, Harrington Park Press, 1991, for a selection of writings from the journal *Der Eigene* (*The Self-Owner*), which outline the theories of the Community of Self-Owners. See also James D. Steakley, *The Homosexual Emancipation Movement in Germany*, Arno Press, 1975.

new stable of patients over whom they could wield their increasingly esoteric knowledge.[40]
2. *Hegemonic.* The division of the human race into two main groups based on sexual tastes reinforced gender stereotypes at a time when movements like feminism and aestheticism were blurring the boundaries between what had hitherto been construed as nature-given roles and behaviours.[41] The effeminacy model maintained the gender *status quo* and reinforced masculine and feminine heterosexuality by suggesting that gender role behaviour was innate.
3. *Tactical.* Homosexuals saw in the medical model a way of defining themselves which did not involve seeing their desire as either sinful or sick; the liberationist potential of arguing that one was 'born that way', however, was rapidly foreclosed by the homophobic theoretical framework available.
4. *Epistemological.* By the mid-nineteenth century the human mind was so enamoured with and shaped by the concept of binary thought that its application in the sexual field was inevitable. The homo/hetero binarism needed recognizably different or opposed categories. Therefore, homosexuals were positioned in stark contrast to traditional heterosexual masculinity in order to reinforce the binary opposition.
5. *Political.* The Self-Owners' tendency to reject the effeminacy model went hand in hand with certain strands of nationalism, misogyny, anti-feminism and right wing politics that rendered their particular brand of homosexual liberation rather unpalatable. Their emphasis on manly strength and comradeship was virtually indistinguishable from the kind of heroism, masculinism and racism that led to Nazism.[42]

---

40 See D.F. Greenberg, *The Construction of Homosexuality*, University of Chicago Press, 1988, 397–399; Colin Spencer, *Homosexuality: A History*, Fourth Estate, 1995, 289–90; L. Birkin, *Consuming Desire: Sexual Science and the Emergence of a Culture of Abundance 1871–1914*, Cornell University Press, 1988, 92–112.

41 See Elaine Showalter, *Sexual Anarchy: Gender and Culture at the Fin de Siècle*, Virago, 1990.

42 The youth movement Wandervogel had close links with the Community of Self-Owners and one of its first members, Hans Bluher, was to become "one of the most important right-wing ideologues of the Mannerbund, propagating a purification of German society" (Oosterhuis & Kennedy, *Homosexuality and Male Bonding in Pre-Nazi Ger-*

6. *Orthodoxical.* The Self-Owners opposed medicine and therefore were speaking, ostensibly, without any authority. There was, in the early years of the 20th century, a great need to see in the medical profession a new order of Faith which, replacing the Church, became the moulder of opinions. Nowhere was this more apparent than in the field of sexuality.[43]
7. *Reformist.* The third sex theory, positing homosexuality as inborn and immutable, best served the emancipationist struggle in Germany against Paragraph 175,[44] and therefore gained the upper hand over the Self-Owners' less essentialist theory. This ensured the durability of the inversion trope despite its failure in opposing anti-homosexual legislation. Medical discourse was a Trojan horse for homosexual emancipationists, who, once through the gates, were not allowed to emerge from the wooden effigy.

Homotopia?

In *The Order of Things* Foucault investigates Western epistemology's insistence on taxonomy, on ordering things through "our age-old distinction between the Same and the Other". He cites a passage from Borges in which 'a certain Chinese encylcopaedia' lists the categorization of animals along the lines of:

(a) belonging to the Emperor, (b) embalmed, (c) tame, (d) suckling pigs, (e) sirens, (f) fabulous, (g) stray dogs, (h) in-

---

many, 123); see also Ian Young, *The Stonewall Experiment,* Cassell, 1995, 42: "A number of prominent homosexual spokesmen of the time […] became racists, associating homosexuality with 'manly purity' and 'Aryan superiority'".

43 One of the members of the Community of Self-Owners, Benedict Friedlander, drew a comparison between medieval priests and early 20th century doctors. Prefiguring Foucault's argument that the religious confession was replaced by medical inquiry, Friedlander wrote in 1907: "Just as doctors live from healing sickness, those medieval priests lived from the forgiveness of sins. Thus, just as the doctor is dependent on the presence of the real or imagined sick person, so too the medieval priest was dependent on the presence of people who held themselves, with or without reason, to be 'sinners'" (Oosterhuis & Kennedy, *Homosexuality and Male Bonding in Pre-Nazi Germany,* 82–3).

44 Paragraph 175 of the German Penal Code, which punished so-called 'vices against nature' with prison sentences, was introduced into the legislation of the German Empire in 1871. See Kennedy, *Ulrichs,* 148–9; Oosterhuis & Kennedy, *Homosexuality and Male Bonding in Pre-Nazi Germany,* 1–21; Lauritsen & Thorstad, *The Early Homosexual Rights Movement,* 6–16; Martin Dannecker, *Theories of Homosexuality,* GMP, 1978, 15–24.

cluded in the present classification, (i) frenzied, (j) innumerable, (k) drawn with a very fine camelhair brush, (l) et cetera, (m) having just broken the water pitcher, (n) that from a long way off look like flies.[45]

Foucault concludes that all taxonomy is arbitrary, a product of thought processes which strive to identify along lines of sameness and difference. This taxonomic process is driven by a desire for comfort, a desire to make sense of the chaos of the world. But it is ultimately Utopic, having "no real locality". A no-place place. But none the less real for all that.

Utopias, Foucault argues, "open up cities with vast avenues, superbly planted gardens, countries where life is easy" (OT, xviii). The opposite scenario he terms Heterotopias, which are "disturbing, probably because they secretly undermine language, because they make it impossible to name this and that, because they shatter or tangle common names, because they destroy 'syntax' in advance, and not only the syntax with which we construct sentences but also that less apparent syntax which causes words and things (next to and also opposite one another) to 'hold together'" (OT, xviii). Whereas utopias "permit fables and discourse", their evil twin, heteropias, serves to "dessicate speech" and "dissolve our myths". But surely the opposite of heterotopia would be homotopia? The chaos of difference versus the harmony of sameness.

The construction of human sexuality into two neat, distinct categories – homosexual and heterosexual – is just such a myth, intended to afford consolation and impose order on the terrifying chaos of human desires. The categorization of the homosexual as a separate type or species with a diacritically marked body is necessary to alleviate the anxiety that would ensue from the possibility of homosexual desire occurring in those not conforming to such morphology. The maintenance of the two categories is contingent upon the representation and promotion of

---
45 Michel Foucault, *The Order of Things: An Archaeology of the Human Sciences*, Vintage Books, 1973, xv. Further citations will appear in the text, indicated by the abbreviation OT.

difference between the two, bordering on subspecies. Such difference extends, as I hope to show, to the categorization within the homosexual paradigm, to the extent that the heterosexual model of male/female informs the reading of homosexual activity: one partner (invariably the penetrator) is male, while the other (penetrated) partner is female. Sexual difference, it seems, haunts even sexual sameness. Positionality is all.

The destruction of the syntax that allows the myth to perpetuate could well be instigated by a refusal to see such a distinction, by an insistance on the sameness (and equality) not only of the two bodies engaged in homosexual sex, but also the radical sameness of heterosexuals to homosexuals, a sameness that democratizes sexuality. Not so much a free for all as a place of true egality, where bodies and pleasures are not locked in violent hierarchies[46] which privilege and proscribe. A place I call *Homotopia*. I use this neologism to name a nexus of definitional concerns at the core of same-sex desire. To inscribe homosexuality as desire without lack, as rather, a form of poesis, "an active intervention, a provocation: an interruption".[47] It is a site of impossibility, unthinkability, but none the less heterotopic. Indeed, it is both utopic and heterotopic in the Foucauldian sense: a chimerical place whose function is to disturb, disrupt, dissolve.

---

46 Jacques Derrida refers to binarisms as 'violent hierarchies' in *Positions*, trans. Alan Bass, Athlone, 1981, 41.
47 William Haver, 'Queer Research: Or, How to Practise Invention to the Brink of Intelligibility', in S. Golding (ed.), *The Eight Technologies of Otherness*, Routledge, 1997, 278.

Chapter One

Against Custom:
André Gide's Pedagogic Pederasty

> "Before discussing, one ought always to define."
> – André Gide, *Journals*

The life of André Gide (1869–1951) remains one of the great coming out narratives in the history of sexuality, showing a courage and honesty about his homosexuality at a time when it didn't pay to be courageous or honest. Yet he was also guilty of prejudice, prudishness, self-interest and self-oppression. This tension represents one of the characteristics of homosexual discourse, a struggle between claims for naturalness and a capitulation to widespread homophobia. Gide's polemic on male–male love, *Corydon,* whilst clearly an example of reverse discourse, is at the same time a profoundly anti-gay text, reviling all forms of homosexuality other than the one Gide himself practiced: pederasty.[1] Of the four texts this book analyses, *Corydon* was the last to be published, and is the starting point of this study because in a sense it constitutes a distillation of the themes of homosexual discourse at the time. Gide began work on it at the turn of the century, and it is possible, therefore, to see in this text the limits of the discourse, the meanings and definitions with which it worked, and the themes with which it dealt.

---

1 For a discussion of pederasty and homosexuality in Gide see Kevin Kopelson, *Love's Litany: The Writing of Modern Homoerotics,* Stanford University Press, 1994. For a more general discussion on man/boy love see Mark Pascal (ed.), *Varieties of Man/Boy Love,* Wallace Hamilton Press, 1992; see also Joseph Geraci (ed.), *Dares To Speak: Historical & Contemporary Perspectives on Boy-Love,* GMP, 1997.

In this chapter, using Gide's *Corydon*, his *Journals,* and the autobiographical *If It Die,* I intend to show how Gide's own paranoia over a particular sexual act fed his theoretical approach to homosexuality and warped his arguments, so that, rather than promote tolerance, he perpetuated stereotypes and fostered greater intolerance, casting aside all forms of same-sex behaviour other than pederasty as deserving social opprobrium, and establishing a model for gay identity based on a refusal of particular sexual acts and expressions and a strict policing of desire which can only be described as homophobic.

How Shall I Address Thee?

Although Gide rejected all the major medico-legal writers, he was clearly influenced by their taxonomic definitions of the various types of homosexual. He formulated his own taxonomy in his *Journals* as follows:

> I call a pederast the man who, as the word indicates, falls in love with young boys. I call a sodomite [...] the man whose desire is addressed to mature men. I call an invert the man who, in the comedy of love, assumes the role of a woman and desires to be possessed[2]

For Gide, then, pederasty is the only form of homosexuality that involves love. Sodomites and inverts merely fuck, perform a "comedy of love". We can conclude from this a separation of love from sex which Gide's own biography dramatizes, and which stereotypes of gay promiscuity maintain. On the one hand, there is love; on the other, sex. There is a denial of the emotional built into Gide's definition of the sodomite and the invert, as there is a denial of or refusal of the sexual built into his definition of the pederast.

And yet the Greek model of pederasty which Corydon champions often involved, as David Halperin points out, "the penetration of the body of one person by the body (and, specifically,

---
2   André Gide, *Journals*, vol. 2, *1914–27,* trans. Justin O'Brien, Secker & Warburg, 1951, 157.

the phallus) of another".[3] Moreover, according to Greek mores, the penetrator should be the social superior to the penetrated. In Greek pederasty, sodomy was performed by free adult men on young boys and slaves, their social inferiors – a fact Gide overlooks. Consider the disgust Corydon displays for sodomy when discussing the appearance of sodomites in Titian's painting, *The Council of Trent*: "It seems bravado, vice, an exceptional amusement for the debauched and the blasé."[4] Sodomy emerges as a behaviour indulged in only by those who have refused standard socialization: the debauched and the blasé, the act itself a vice, a vaunted display of courage.

By not acknowledging that what he terms 'Greek love' was commonly expressed through anal intercourse, Gide is not only being inaccurate, he is being disingenuous.[5] Moreover, Corydon claims to dislike inverts because "their defect is too evident" and "poorly informed people confuse normal homosexuals with them" (C, 119), something which would not happen, Gide believed, if they knew that different *types* of homosexual existed. And for Gide, only certain types deserved equality. Following on from the previous extract from his *Journals,* he writes:

> These three types of homosexual are not always clearly distinct: there are possible transferences from one to another; but most often the difference among them is such that they experience a profound disgust for one another, a disgust accompanied by a reprobation that in no way yields to that which you (heterosexuals) fiercely show toward all three.

---

[3] David Halperin, 'Is There a History of Sexuality?', in H. Abelove et al. (eds), *The Lesbian and Gay Studies Reader*, Routledge, 1993, 418.
[4] André Gide, *Corydon* [1924], trans. Richard Howard, GMP, 1983, 18. All subsequent page references will appear in the text indicated by the abbreviation C.
[5] It seems unlikely, given Gide's knowledge of ancient Greece, that he was not aware of this. One can only put it down to personal distaste. It's worth remembering that 'urning' or 'uranian' was the neologism penned by Ulrichs to describe the type of homosexual who suffered from feminization of that part of the psyche which dictated sexual appetite, causing him to desire men just like a heterosexual woman does. It was also the theoretical foundation for Hirschfeld's Third Sex. Gide's use of it as a synonym for 'homosexual' throughout *Corydon* is therefore inconsistent with his loathing for effeminacy and Third Sexism.

What these transferences might be (much less what Gide's own experience of them was) are not revealed, though it's apparent that Gide, transferences notwithstanding, wishes to maintain the barriers of disgust between the three types. Furthermore, he accuses the inverts of being the bad apples by which the entire crop is judged, their effeminacy justifying the opprobrium and disgust heaped upon them, not least for the fact that by it all homosexuals are tainted: "It has always seemed to me that they alone deserved the reproach of moral or intellectual deformation and were subject to some of the accusations that are commonly addressed to all homosexuals."

In the light of such comments, we must view *Corydon* as being strictly concerned with Gide's own specific sexual preference, and not as a defense for homosexual behaviour *per se* in all its varied and glorious manifestations. For example, footnoted in the preface to the third edition of *Corydon*, Gide expresses his dissatisfaction with Hirschfeld's Third Sex theory:

> The theory of the woman-man, of the Sexuelle Zwischenstufen, (intermediate degrees of sexuality) advanced by Dr. Hirschefeld in Germany […] and which Marcel Proust appears to accept – may well be true enough; but that theory explains and concerns only certain cases of homosexuality, precisely those with which this book does not deal – cases of inversion, effeminacy, of sodomy (C, xx)

We are thus informed what the book isn't about; what Gide isn't going to discuss. Yet he concedes, in the same footnote, that his omission of these topics is "one of [his] book's great shortcomings", because "they turn out to be much more frequent than [he] previously supposed"(C, xx), although their omission is justified on the grounds that:

> Even granting that Hirschfeld's theory accounts for these cases, his 'third sex' argument certainly cannot explain what we

habitually call 'greek love': pederasty – having not the slightest element of effeminacy on either side.[6]

This positions Gide's main focus of interest – pederasty – in opposition to the 'third sex' argument, which defined the homosexual as an effeminate man-woman. Yet what remains as conceptually inconceivable to Gide as to the sexologists he wishes to refute, is the same-sex relationship between two adult men; much less sodomy between two without one of them being perceived as a woman *manqué*. The impetus to locate desire in a theory of difference renders the sameness of same-sex desire invisible: it must always be reducible to difference, be it of age, social position, race or psychology. Furthermore, by denying love to all but pederasts he is revealing what little he knows about love. A love between equals can never be the outcome of a relationship such as pederasty which relies on disequilibrium for its very existence and has a built-in obsolescence in the fact that at the point of maturity the boy's desire is meant to be diverted to women. In addition, Gide's passion for boys sits at odds with Corydon's claim for 'virile homosexuality', for, strictly speaking, 'virility' refers only to adult males.

A Hybrid Production

The third edition of *Corydon*, published in 1924, was the first public edition. *Dialogues* I and II and part of III had appeared in a small private edition in 1911, and in full in a 1920 private edition, both anonymously, and both largely unread (indeed, the 1911 print run of twelve copies were secreted in a drawer[7]). Subtitled 'Four Socratic Dialogues', Corydon takes the form of a dialogue between an unnamed narrator and Dr. Corydon, who is preparing a book on pederasty. Patrick Pollard calls it "a hybrid production in that it stands midway between a work of im-

---

6 Howard translates this as "in which effeminacy is neither here nor there". Patrick Pollard, however, translates it as "having not the slightest effeminacy on either side" (*André Gide: Homosexual Moralist*, Yale University Press, 1991, 27). I prefer the latter, and on this ocassion have vered from Howard's version.

7 Gide, *Journals*, 2.11.

agination and one of documentary fact".[8] Certainly, we can see it as an intervention into a medical discourse which up till that point had disappointed and dissatisfied Gide by promoting the notion of homosexuality as sick and *contra naturam*, examining specimens of the phenomenon found in mental hospitals or doctor's consulting rooms. In order to refute the Third Sex theory, Gide takes great pains to assure us that Corydon is in no way effeminate: his dress is conventional, even austere (*C*, 4) and his (heterosexual) interlocutor searches in vain for signs of "that effeminacy which experts manage to discover in everything connected with inverts and by which they claim they are never deceived". Gide deliberately opposes accepted medical doctrine because, as Pollard explains, "so pervasive was the influence of the writers of the medico-legal works and text books of sexual and mental hygiene that it was as important for Gide to demolish their general credibility as to argue on purely moral grounds the particular case of boy love which was his real concern".[9] Yet, by singling out pederasty as "his main concern", Gide contributed to the taxonomic process, supplying another category and reinforcing the intolerance directed at those types which by the time Gide's book appeared had become all too familiar.

Foucault's work on the nineteenth century *scientia sexualis* helps elucidate the taxonomic operation by which sexual diversity was both recognized and proscribed – indeed, recognized in order to be proscribed; what Foucault calls an "incorporation of perversions" and a "specification of individuals". Each behavioural characteristic was seen as a different form of sexuality, even a different sexuality – "all those minor perverts whom nineteenth-century psychiatrists entomologized by giving them strange baptismal names" were no more than representatives of various points along a continuum of human sexual expression. The law and medicine – "the machinery of power" – needed a way to control this diversity of undefined sexualities and to this end, there emerged a formalized and finely-categorised science constructed around sexual behaviours, gestures and experienc-

---

8   Pollard, *André Gide*, 11.
9   Patrick Pollard, 'Andre Gide and his Adversaries', in *European Gay Review* 4 (1989), 85.

es, giving them an "analytical, visible and permanent reality". This reality was inaugurated via medical enquiry: "imbedded in bodies, becoming deeply characteristic of individiuals, the oddities of sex relied on a technology of health and pathology". In this way, Foucault argues, power was extended to actual, individual bodies, and an intimate surveillance was established and maintained: "scattered sexualities rigidified, became stuck to an age, a place, a type of practice" (*HS*, 43–44).[10]

According to Foucault, there is no reason to see any sexuality as a true identity category or an expression of an inner, pre-discursive self. Rather, sexualities are constantly called into being, constantly changing, and constantly altering the nature of sexual discourse. Sexual identity, he suggests, has become a self-imposed mechanism of social control. Yet at the same time, identity has become the only way to make sense of one's desires. The problem arises when certain identities are promoted and validated whilst others remain marginalized and despised. Social control has been necessary to recognize and proscribe sexual behaviours deemed unacceptable. With equality for all forms of desire, wouldn't such social control become redundant?

Within sexological discourse, the only concept for theorizing male–male love very quickly became the inversion model, by which one partner, invariably the receptive partner during anal intercourse, was cast as a woman: he was the innate homosexual. The insertive partner was invariably seen as not an innate homosexual; his desire aligned much more with the 'acquired'

---

10 In France the plight of the homosexual was not so much legal as social. In 1791 sex between consenting men was decriminalized, although with minors it was still illegal. Copley asks whether the leniency of the French legal system on the issue of sex between men can be seen to have inhibited or weakened the emergence of a "self-conscious homosexual movement" (Anthony Copley, *Sexual Moralities in France 1780–1980*, Routledge, 1989, 135). Whereas in England and Germany the struggle for law reform gave such movements their *raison d'être*, in France there was no such contrafugal point of resistance. Copley does point out, however, that the regulation of public decency offences in France approximated that in England, so the difference in cultures need not be too exaggerated. In both countries, the medical profession rose in stature and gained political power in the last quarter of the nineteenth century.

model. In 1857, Tardieu claimed to be able to recognize a passive homosexual by examining the anus.[11]

A distinct identity was thus constructed upon the fact of a particular sexual act. But identities are no less real for being historically or socially constructed.[12] If homosexuals responded positively to the medical appellation at the end of the last century it was because it appealed to a need for discursive visibility, for coherent identity, regardless of sexual positioning: indeed, Gide is a case in point. Attracted by the opportunity to explain his desires within a biologistic register, he nevertheless refused the medical diagnosis of sickness.

By actually excluding inversion, which up to that point had been the central trope of same-sex behaviour within medical discourse, Gide was not only redressing the balance, presenting same-sex behaviour from his own perspective (as a lover of boys), he was also challenging the medical assumption that the Ulrichsian inversion model accounted for all, or even a large part, of cases of homosexuality.

As early as 1894 Gide was expressing a dissatisfaction with medical accounts of homosexuality. After reading Moll's book, *Les Perversions de l'instinct genital,* he wrote to a friend:

> He does not differentiate enough between two classes: the effeminate men and the others – he constantly mixes them together, and nothing is more different, more contrary – because one is opposed to the other – because for that kind of psychophysiology, that which does not attract repels – and each horrifies the other.[13]

The horror is patently Gide's own, and not a psychophysiological phenomenon. Less sophisticated than the taxonomics of the

---

11 Alain Corbin, 'Backstage', in M. Perrot (ed.), *A History of Private Life,* vol. 4: *From the Fires of Revolution to the Great War,* Belknap Press of Harvard University Press, 1990, 640.

12 Jeffrey Weeks, 'Questions of Identity', in *Against Nature: Essays on History, Sexuality and Identity,* Rivers Oram Press, 1981, 84.

13 Unpublished letter to a friend, quoted in Jean Delay, *The Youth of André Gide,* trans. June Guichamaud, University of Chicago Press, 1963, 425.

1918 journal entry, he here recognizes only two categories, "the effeminate men and the others". Clearly unhappy about being grouped together with effeminate men, Gide theorizes a 'kind of psychophysiology' that renders both groups mutually horrified and repelled because "nothing is more different, more contrary". As his journal entry makes clear, he regarded effeminate men as deserving of the opprobrium heaped upon them, while "the others" alone are worthy of respect and tolerance, a remarkably intolerant attitude.

Part of Gide's brief was to take male–male love out of the clinic and to present arguments in defense of pederasty that had nothing to do with a "technology of health and pathology". Corydon informs his interlocutor, "the only serious books I know on this subject are certain medical works which reek of the clinic from the very first pages", and complains that "the doctors who usually write about the subject treat only uranists who are ashamed of themselves – pathetic inverts, sick men. They're the ones who consult doctors" (C, 17–18).

Ironically, in 1895, aged twenty five, Gide consulted a neurologist prior to marrying Madeleine Rondeaux.[14] To what extent he confessed his homosexual behaviour or desire he does not say, but the doctor seemed not to share Gide's anxiety and reassured him that marriage would cure him. It would be reasonable to assume that Gide recalled this consultation when employing the Abbe Galiani's quotation in *Corydon*: "the important thing is not to be cured but to be able to live with one's disease" (C, 13). Certainly, the fact that Gide acted so unquestioningly on his doctor's advice suggests a deference to medical authority which, although it was to lessen with age, never fully disappeared.

Perhaps it was in order to avoid the accusation of disease that Gide demonized sodomites and inverts and idealized pederasts. Homosexuality, in Gide's work, appears both within a sickness paradigm and a health paradigm, seriously problematizing his claim for either.

---

14 André Gide, *Et nunc manet in te,* trans. Justin O'Brien, New York: Knopf, 1952, 94.

Face to face

In *If It Die* Gide recounts a scene of anal intercourse between his friend Daniel B. and a young Arab boy, Mohammed (Delay writes "between a sodomite and an invert"[15] in a misapplication of Gide's own taxonomics):

> Daniel seized Mohammed in his arms and carried him over to the bed at the far end of the room. He laid him on his back across the edge of the bed, and soon all I could see was two thin legs dangling on either side of the panting Daniel, who hadn't even taken off his cloak. Very tall, standing against the bed, in semi-darkness, seen from the back, his face hidden by his long black curly hair, in this cloak that came down to his feet, Daniel looked gigantic leaning over this little body which he hid from view.[16]

The passage is significant for its obsession with what is hidden from view. The only light in the room is a solitary candle, and Daniel's cloak[17] veils the spectacle of anal penetration from Gide's gaze, as Daniel's hair hides his face (which would reveal pleasure, no doubt). Anal intercourse is thus something Gide is left to imagine, rather than witness. And his imagination runs riot. With Gothic hyperbole, he compares Daniel to a huge parasitic form, a vampire (always an anti-social, outlaw figure[18]) feasting on his prey (note how Gide exaggerates the comparative sizes of the two men: Daniel is described as gigantic, towering over Mohammed's little body). But what horrifies him just as much as Daniel's unsublimated desire for the anus is Mohammed's willingness to be penetrated:

---

15 Delay, *The Youth of André Gide*, 426.
16 Andre Gide, *If It Die* [1926], trans. Dorothy Bussy, Penguin, 1977, 298. Further citations will appear in the text indicated by the abbreviation *IID*.
17 See Michael Lucey, *Gide's Bent*, Oxford University Press, 1995, 28–29, for a discussion of Gide's attitude to clothes, nudity and sex. See also Emily Apter, 'Homotextual Counter-Codes: Andre Gide & the Poetics of Engagement', in *Michigan Romance Studies* 6, 1986, 75–87.
18 For a discussion of homosexuality and vampirism see Carolyn Brown, 'Figuring the Vampire: death, desire and the image' in Golding (ed.), *The Eight Technologies of Otherness*, 117–33.

As for myself, who can only conceive pleasure face to face, reciprocal and gentle, and who, like Whitman, find satisfaction in the most furtive contact, I was horrified both by Daniel's way of going at it and by the willing cooperation of Mohammed.[19]

Gide cannot comprehend why two men would want to do this. He states, "We always find it hard to understand other people's love-life, their ways of making love" (*IID*, 286). Yet there is no attempt at understanding here, only blind antipathy ("I could have screamed in horror"). Note how Gide's own penchant – for pleasure face to face – is opposed to sodomy, which in this matrix, would be "back to front" (despite the fact that Daniel has laid Mohammed on his back, thus rendering the two men face to face). Irrespective of positioning, use of the anus is seen as antithetical to the mutuality that Gide requires. As Michael Lucey writes, "Fucking represents an excess Gide's fantasy cannot absorb, a form of pleasure he will not imagine as just sexual; it must also be political."[20] According to Lucey, the decadence of Daniel and Mohammed's sex leaves Gide's own furtive contact egalitarian and beyond reproach. To refuse fucking is to refuse seeing sex as political; Gide's own pleasures are saved from a politicizing discourse that might render them suspect. As Guy Hocquenghem argues, the anus is private, hidden, anti-social while the phallus is public, social, visible.[21]

In Leo Bersani's reading of the final scene in Jean Genet's *Funeral Rites*, in which two men fuck doggy style on a rooftop in Paris (i.e., not Gide's preferred face to face), their positioning renders homosexual intercourse intractably anti-social, for it privileges, for Bersani at least, individual sexual *pleasure* over shared sexual *intimacy*. He argues that the intimacy of a mutual

---

[19] Gide, *If It Die*, 287. The original French is "... de voir s'y preter aussi complaisament Mohammed", which translates best as "willing cooperation", although Lucey translates it as "by seeing Mohammed go along with it so complacently". Complacency is not the same thing as willingness, and for my argument Mohammed's desire/pleasure is crucial, which is not connoted by Lucey's translation.

[20] Lucey, *Gide's Bent*, 37.

[21] Guy Hocquenghem, *Homosexual Desire*, trans. Danielle Dangoor, Duke University Press, 1993, 96. See the conclusion of this book for a more detailed account of his work.

gaze is required by our culture for ultimate privacy and intimate knowledge of the other, an intimacy upon which "the familial cell is built". Thus sodomy "takes on the value of a break or seismic shift in a culture's episteme: the injunction to find ourselves, and each other, in the sexual".[22] Traditional phrases like 'sexual intercourse', 'sexual congress', 'sexual union', suggest a sharing or conjoining of souls, a bonding that is starkly at odds with Bersani's reading of Genet, in which buggery emerges as the opposite of such sharing or bonding: it is, rather, the refusal of it. By seeing Daniel and Mohammed's coupling as antithetical to his own face to face pleasures, Gide would seem to be projecting onto this act a similarly radical and socially destabilizing potentiality.

How much more destabilizing, though, if it were the other way around, Mohammed sodomizing Daniel, the colonized colonizing the colon of the colonizer? Or, perish the thought, if love were involved? If, rather than being seen as anti-relational, sodomy between men were an expression of that intimacy Bersani wants to refute. After all, of whom is that intimacy demanded? Not gay people, surely, against whom the stereotype of anonymous, promiscuous, loveless sexual encounters is all too often employed. As Foucault has suggested, it's not so much the idea of gay sex that is socially unacceptable but the idea of two men achieving happiness together, of formulating new types of personal relationships.[23] This could also go some way to explaining Gide's excessive disgust at the sight of Daniel and Mohammed going at it hammer and tongs. Perhaps it is that very intimacy that sodomy requires which Gide finds so distasteful. It is a meeting of two equal forces in a rather violently passionate manner that makes him almost scream in horror. Gide could not equate sex with love and therefore refused to equate sex with intimacy. Recounting his own encounter with Mohammed two years earlier, he writes, "My joy was unbounded, and I cannot imagine it greater, even if love had been added. How could love have entered into this? How could I have left my heart at the mercy

---

22 Leo Bersani, *Homos*, Harvard University Press, 1995, 165.
23 Quoted in ibid., 77.

of my desire?" (*IID*, 284). Gide was clearly terrified of emotional vulnerability, to the point where he was unable, or unwilling, to allow himself to feel any emotion other than physical pleasure, and then, after the boy's departure, Gide masturbated repeatedly to the point of numb exhaustion, because when one is exhausted one can feel nothing but one's exhaustion.

The fact that Mohammed had been Gide's partner in pederasty two years prior to being Daniel's in sodomy does not lead Gide to reflect on the instability and possible futility of such identity categories as sodomite or pederast; rather, it makes him all the more determined to maintiain those barriers of disgust referred to earlier. Neither does it occur to him that Mohammed is in a subservient position to colonials like Gide and Daniel B, rendering him obliged to respond to their sexual demands: he is a prostitute.

In *If It Die* Gide writes: "We always find it hard to understand other people's love-life, their ways of making love [...] nothing is so disconcerting as the methods, varying so much from species to species, by which each of them finds his pleasure" (*IID*, 286). Coming as it does after the scene in which Daniel sodomizes Mohammed, we can see here a dramatization of Foucault's claim that while the sodomite had been an aberration, the homosexual – via medicalization – became a species (*HS*, 43). Under Gide's essentializing gaze what is no more than a sexual act becomes a personality type, a species. The fact that the same body (Mohammed's) can engage itself at one time in pederastic practices (according to Delay, Gide went no further than mutual masturbation[24]) and at another time in sodomy, significantly undermines any theory (such as sexology) that would base identity on behaviour. Gide contradicts himself, shifting as he does between an insistence on essentialist notions of authenticity and selfhood and a desire to discredit those medical theories that would see in the homosexual a distinct and essential personality type. Gide wrote in his *Journals*, "desire loses all value and does not deserve to be taken into consideration the moment it ceases to be in

---

24 Delay, *The Youth of André Gide*, 440–1.

harmony with, and similar to, [heterosexuals]".[25] Yet is he not a victim of the same prejudice when faced with a form of desire not in harmony with his own? Is his intolerance of sodomites any different to society's hatred of all homosexuals, of which he is highly critical? And what 'makes' a sodomite, anyway? Is it an act or an identity? Or, following Judith Butler, is it the repetition of acts parading as an identity? Moreover, in Bersani's words, "How does the wish to repeat pleasurable stimulations of the body translate into, or come to constitute, intersubjectivity?"[26]

Mohammed's fluctuation between sodomy and pederasty presents Gide with an incomprehensibly fluid model of desire, one which causes those barriers of disgust of which he is so fond to come crashing down around his ears.

An Entirely Human Invention

In *The Youth of Andre Gide,* Jean Delay reassures us that Gide's was not an innate homosexuality, "and therefore fatal, but acquired, and therefore modifiable".[27] Delay's diagnosis is based on the fact that Gide was not effeminate, whereas for Delay an innate homosexual dreams, feels and loves like a woman due to his over-identification with a mother who is extremely feminine, "thus very different from Mme. Paul Gide".[28] Delay thus overlooks Gide's own affirmative statements on his acceptance of his true nature – "I now found what was normal in me" – and instead laments the passing of Gide's opportunity to be heterosexual.

This judgemental attitude renders Delay incapable of seeing Gide as anything other than flawed or damaged and in need of a cure: "He had a homosexuality neurosis […] which is susceptible of medical treatment, at least today"[29]; an attitude wildly at odds with Gide's own view. He also ignores Gide's confession in *If It Die* that in order to achieve intercourse with the Arab girl Meriem he imagined he was holding a boy, Mohammed (*IID,* 255) – interesting, given Gide's loathing for male penetration.

---

25 Gide, *Journals,* 2.214.
26 Bersani, *Homos,* 60.
27 Delay, *The Youth of André Gide,* 60.
28 Ibid., 441.
29 Ibid., 396. Delay offers no evidence to support this claim, because there isn't any.

What he imagined doing to Mohammed whilst fucking Meriem is anyone's guess.

In Delay's account, effeminacy emerges as the signal factor defining the innate homosexual. For Gide, as we have seen, effeminate homosexuals are the most loathsome, and his reason is clear: they are passive sodomites, taking the role of the woman in intercourse; as such, they are not male, but a Third Sex. Gide therefore ends up supporting and promoting the theory he set out to contest. According to *Corydon,* procreation cannot be regarded as the primary motor for sexual intercourse; rather, it is a byproduct. The principle motivation is pleasure. Pleasure thus becomes a human universal truth (much like Freud's libido) possessing the potential to reduce intolerance of the varying ways in which others choose to obtain theirs.

Gide's own tolerance of the ways some other people choose to obtain their pleasure, as we have seen, was sometimes slim. Anal intercourse, for example, was not within Gide's scope of understanding or tolerance. For Corydon, sodomy is "an exceptional amusement for the debauched and the blasé" (C, 89). An amusement much less exceptional, however, than Gide first imagined, as he concedes in his journal entry of 1918, where he claims that pederasts are "much rarer, and the sodomites much more numerous, than I first thought".[30]

Corydon's argument that procreation is a by-product of the pursuit of pleasure ("The animal seeks pleasure – and finds fertilization by accident" [C, 36]) rests on the dubious (and phallocentric) premise that while females can only participate in intercourse at certain periods (i.e. when they are on heat), males are willing and able to perform at all times, which is why they often indulge in homosexual activity when no females are ovulating.

Not only does this 'any-port-in-a-storm' argument, by which desire becomes some sex-blind, free-floating instinct for gratification regardless of object, run counter to the notion of sexual volition or preference (not to mention its complete omission of any form of lesbianism) upon which he aims to base his de-

---

30 Gide, *Journals,* 2.158.

fense of pederasty; but it is also seriously compromised by his later call for greater self-control over sexual appetite. *Corydon* is concerned with showing how heterosexuality is socially constructed as an absolute and exclusive condition for the health and perpetuation of the human race, and as such he argues it is custom rather than nature that is being violated by homosexual behaviour: "Where you say 'against nature' the phrase 'against custom' would do" (C, 27). It is customary for men to have sex with (and impregnate) women, and Corydon argues that an entire psychology (love) has been constructed around this one physical act and qualified its status as 'natural' to the extent that any other form of sexual behaviour is deemed 'unnatural' precisely because it goes against this custom. Yet man himself, not nature, has drawn the boundary lines over which it is deemed unnatural to transgress: "Love is an entirely human invention – it does not exist in a state of nature" (C, 33).

Gide employs, in *Corydon*, a double-edged meaning of 'nature', which not only incorporates the natural world but also the idea of a true and essential self ('one's nature'). Given the second sense of the word, to go against nature would be to deny one's homosexual impulse, while admitting them and acting on them is part of an acceptance of what is one's true nature. In Algiers, following the acceptance of his homosexual desire, Gide wrote to his mother: "I should like very submissively to follow nature – the unconscious, which is within myself and must be true", suggesting the existence of an essential, unshakably 'true' self which his transgression of sexual conformity has liberated.

This 'essential' self would appear to be an original, prediscursive plenitude to which it is necessary to return if one is to maintain an authentic identity. At the same time, that he wishes "very submissively to follow" this nature denies any autonomy. In the light of such an admission, just how radical is Gide's essentialism?

A Radical Essentialism?

To acknowledge an essential homosexuality within oneself as Gide did was to go some way towards conceding the concept of innateness, which is something Corydon seems both to accept and resist.[31] Accept in as much as Corydon argues against the theory of an acquired homosexuality: "When he imitates it's because he wants to imitate [...] the example corresponded to his secret preference" (*C*, 30); resist in the sense that Corydon suggests homosexuality "can scarcely be inherited for the plausible reason that the very act which would transmit it is necessarily a heterosexual act" (*C*, 30. Ellipsis in original). Yet no one knew better than Gide that in order to procreate one didn't need to be heterosexual, for he had a daughter himself by a woman other than his wife.

This points to a separation of act from identity which Gide was incapable of in his reading of Daniel and Mohammed's fuck scene. He may be willing to divorce pleasure from procreation but cannot, it seems, divorce preference from essence. In *Corydon* at least, participation in a particular sexual activity, even if only for a short period of time – as in the case of pederasty, where the adolescent, upon reaching his majority, should switch, and be perfectly suited to, heterosexual marriage – would seem to involve an alignment between that activity and the desires of an essential self, or identity. Except that Gide is not interested in the identity or essence of the boys with whom he has sex. His focus is on his own nature and the coherence he can acquire for it.

Leo Bersani argues that Gide's sexuality is anti-social or anti-relational because of this disinterest in his partners. Indeed, taking his cue from Foucault, in an interview where he stated that homosexuality is capable of "inventing new possibilities of pleasure with strange parts of [the body]", Bersani sees Gide's account of homosexuality as "more threatening to dominant cultural ideologies" than, for example, an account which included anal penetration. This is because "not only does it play dangerously with the terms of a sexual relation (active and passive, dominant and submissive) – it eliminates from 'sex' *the necessity of any relation whatsoever*".[32]

---

31   For a discussion of radical essentialism see Diana Fuss, *Essentially Speaking: Feminism, Nature and Difference*, Routledge, 1989.
32   Bersani, *Homos*, 122. Original emphasis.

Bersani's citation of the scene in *The Immoralist* where Michel gets off on touching the Arab boy Bachir's "delicate shoulder" would certainly be an example of taking pleasure from "strange parts of the body", but where does this lead us in an analysis of homosexuality? Whilst acknowledging that Gidean homosexuality is 'indistinguishable from a homophobic rejection of sex",[33] Bersani sees in this anti-relationality a radical potential to see all homosexuality as anti-social because, in its emphasis on sameness, it oblates the discursive command for difference in sexual relationships. I agree with Bersani's conclusion, though remain unconvinced by his example of Gide's refusal of a directly sexual relationship with Arab boys, or, when sex does occur, Gide's refusal to recognize his partners as equals.

Take Gide's hatred of inverts. It seems clear that he sees their desires as dependent on difference, with one partner acting the role of a man and the other of a woman. Man and woman are fixed terms in this analysis, and only pederasty can avoid such heterosexualization of same-sex behaviour. But his exclusive interest in young Arab men and boys is just as involved in notions of difference, in this case transgenerational and racial.

By concentrating so much on excavating his own 'true self', Gide renders himself incapable of relating to or considering others. He could thus be accused of pure essentialism, his concept of the sexual self allowing no room for personal volition or change, and ignoring the social factors in the constitution of human sexuality. He wrote to a friend: "I have not chosen to be thus. I can struggle against my desires, I can overcome them, but I cannot choose the object of these desires nor invent others by imitation […]. I have never felt any desire towards a woman."[34] In Gide's account, we are all subject to an essential, true nature which it is our task to unearth, understand and, ultimately, to express. Is this radical?

Jonathan Dollimore believes so: "For Gide transgression is in the name of a desire and identity rooted in the natural, the

---

33 Ibid., 121.
34 Gide in a letter to Claudel, quoted in Enid Starkie, *Gide*, Bowes & Bowes, 1953, 89.

sincere, and the authentic."[35] Contrasting Gide's position with Wilde's anti-essentialism, Dollimore sees in Gide's method of appropriating dominant concepts such as 'the normal' and 'the natural' to legitimate his own deviation a kind of willful perversity in the service of a radical sexual essentialism: "in Gide we find essentialism in the service a radical sexual nonconformity which was and remains largely outlawed by conventional and dominant sexual ideologies, be they bourgeois or socialist". Dollimore uses Gide's 'unified subject' to argue against postmodernism's insistence that essentialism has always been the exclusive property of dominant ideologies; always conservative, never subversive. The fact that the category of the 'natural' is so central to the dominant culture forces subcultures to appropriate it in their struggle for legitimacy. For Dollimore, Gide "conjoins self-authenticity and sexual dissidence" in the name of a radical politics of desire.

Transgressive desire does not, for Gide, lead to a shattering of self but to a consolidation of what one truly is. The ultimate task is to discover one's essential, authentic nature: "a new self created from liberated desire".[36] And consequential to the disclosure of this new self is the excavation, within that self, of "the tables of a new law" (*IID*, 298). Like Michel in *The Immoralist,* after discovering his true nature Gide renounces his old, false self in favour of this new, liberated one. Such a model of sexuality immediately suggests Foucault's critique of the category of sexuality as a discursive and disciplinary product: "sexuality must not be thought of as a kind of natural given which power tries to hold in check, or as an obscure domain which knowledge tries gradually to uncover" (*HS*, 105).Rather it should be thought of as a category through which the will to truth can activate a strategy for political power.

The true sex which Gide is so anxious to excavate is, in Foucauldian terms, not the cause but the *effect* of the very discursive impulse which forces Gide to pursue it. Gide's essentializing of

---
35 Jonathan Dollimore, *Sexual Dissidence: Augustine to Wilde, Freud to Foucault,* Oxford University Press, 1991, 14.
36 Ibid., 13; 26.

his own particular brand of same-sex desire thus, by the same token, also essentializes those categories he disclaims in the preface to Corydon, and it becomes impossible to salvage Gide for a radicalism he clearly doesn't possess.

Unlike Wilde, for whom the idea of a true self was preposterous, Gide accepted that one has an essential and discoverable self or nature to which one must always be true. Gide was terrified of Wilde precisely because he felt his own beliefs – his own self – under threat in Wilde's presence.[37] Rather than, as Wilde did, refute the existence of an authentic self, Gide preferred to appropriate it and inscribe his own homosexual identity within that prevailing discourse. Not content with simply breaking with conformity, he felt the need to vindicate his nonconformity, drawing on the realm of nature to support his claim for sexual authenticity.

As he writes in *If It Die,* "Emancipation from rule did not suffice me; I boldly claimed to justify my folly, to base my madness upon reason" (*IID,* 298). His main justification of his folly was *Corydon,* in which he refutes concepts such as degeneracy and vice in favour of health and self-control; a stylistics of existence based on the Greek model of *ascesis.*[38]

Richard Howard grandly claims that "*Corydon* remains one of the books crucial to an understanding of the development of the Western mind in the first quarter of the twentieth century."[39] If we can make sense of that statement at all, it would be in the context of binary thinking, which Gide both maintains – in the case of inverts, sodomites, etc – and also challenges by insisting on healthy uranism. This tradition of attacking and defending binarisms has marked our century's thinking, particularly on

---

37 See Jonathan Fryer, *André and Oscar: Gide, Wilde and the Gay Art of Living,* Constable, 1997. See also Dollimore, *Sexual Dissidence.*

38 For more on ascesis see Foucault, *The History of Sexuality,* vol. 2: *The Use of Pleasure,* trans. Robert Hurley, Penguin, 1984. See also Halperin, *Saint Foucault.*

39 Richard Howard, 'From Exoticism to Homosexuality', in G. Stambolian and E. Marks, (eds), *Homosexualities and French Literature: Cultural Contexts/Critical Texts,* Cornell University Press, 1979, 324. Gide considered *Corydon* to be his most important and useful book, as well as the one he felt least attracted to and the one with which he found the most fault. He called it "the token of a release", adding: "And who can tell the number of those whom that little book has, likewise, released?"

the contentious site of sexuality. We can see it as one of the strategies by which reverse discourse functions, for reverse discourse is not separate from the discourse it reverses; they are part and parcel of the same field of knowledge. By necessity, they share knowledge in a battle to secure meanings and concepts: the same theoretical tools are taken up both to attack and to defend. It is through this sustained conflict that those meanings and concepts stick, and subsequently make sense of the world.

As Aron and Kempf have noted, "medicine can afford the luxury of cynicism and declare coldly that it is bound only to the principle of objectivity, even if untutored". Medicine, they claim, was far ahead of literature on the issue of homosexuality because doctors are beyond reproach or suspicion, and therefore "can speak of filth without fear of getting [...] dirty".[40] Gide's own fear of getting dirty extended to loathing any form of sex which would expose him to dirt. So he made his defender of healthy uranism a doctor and distanced himself from practices such as effeminacy and sodomy, thus perpetuating the cultural conflation of the two terms along the most homophobic and misogynistic lines.

Given that Gide's rejection of the 'third sex' model in the preface to *Corydon* refers explicitly to Proust's *Sodom et Gomorrhe* as not only being responsible for making the public more accustomed to homosexuality, but also for promoting the notion that homosexuals constitute a third sex, we might ask why the Third Sex model was capable of making homosexuality more palatable. Why was it that Proust's *hommes–femmes* were more socially acceptable and culturally visible than Gide's healthy uranians? What function did it serve in the construction of the homosexual as a discursive figure? To answer these questions, the next chapter explores Proust's theories – theories which in many ways dovetail those of Gide.

---

40 Jean-Paul Aron and Roger Kempf, 'Triumphs and Tribulations of the Homosexual Discourse', in Stambolian & Marks, *Homosexualities and French Literature*, 146.

Chapter Two

No Such Things as Homosexuals:
Marcel Proust and 'La race maudite'

"*The most important perversion, homosexuality, hardly deserves the name.*"
– Sigmund Freud

"*... what is sometimes, most ineptly, termed homosexuality.*"
– Marcel Proust

Although Marcel Proust (1871–1922) never published a pseudo-scientific tract on homosexuality, as such, there is sufficient evidence[1] to support the claim that the opening pages of the volume of *Sodome et Gomorrhe* – that section generally referred

---

1   In a letter to his friend Louise d'Albufera in 1908, Proust listed eight projects on which he was proposing to work: "a study of the nobility; a Parisian novel; an essay on Sainte-Beuve and Flaubert; an essay on women; an essay on pederasty (not easy to publish); a study of stained-glass windows; a study of tombstones; a study of the novel." As Hayman has suggested, "the list [...] should not be taken to mean that the novel, the four studies and the three essays were being planned as eight separate pieces of writing" (*Proust: A Biography,* Heinemann, 1990, 282), and it is more than likely that the essay on pederasty found its way into *A la recherche du temps perdu.* Several writers, including the biographer George Painter, have argued that the first chapter of *Sodome et Gomorrhe,* as well as the chapter in *Contre Sainte-Beuve* entitled 'La race maudite', are examples of Proust 'recasting material originally intended for publication as a non-fiction essay" (J.E. Rivers, *Proust and the Art of Love,* Columbia University Press, 1980, 153). Philip Thody groups it with several other long passages in the novel "which could without much difficulty have been published in essay form" (*Marcel Proust,* MacMillan, 1987, 71–2), albeit, in his view, "a kind of detachable essay in autobiographical guilt." Eve Kosofsky Sedgwick has called it "a thicket of pseudo-scientific self-contradiction" ('Tales of the Avunculate', in *Tendencies,* Routledge, 1994, 59), whilst Leo Bersani dispraises it for its "banal thematization [...] at once sentimental and reductive" ('"The Culture of Redemption": Marcel Proust and Melanie Klein', *Critical Inquiry* 12.2 [Winter 1986], 416). In an early study of Proust, one critic suggests it "should have been entirely cut out" (F.C. Green, *The Mind of Proust,* Cambridge University Press, 1949, 187). We are clearly walking in a minefield here.

to as 'La race maudite' – started life as a non-fictional essay, later inserted into the wider fictional structure of Proust's long novel, *A la recherche du temps perdu*.[2] I shall take as axiomatic this claim that 'La race maudite' began as a non-fictional essay and approach it as such, with a full understanding of the problematics this involves, and despite the fact that the fictional trajectories of some of the homosexual characters from Proust's novel stand in complete contradiction to the ideas about homosexuality expounded in this essay. Indeed, I would argue that this essay capitulates to the medical status quo in a way which significantly contains and defuses any transgressive potential found elsewhere in the novel. Moreover, these few pages most probably serve to consolidate a power the novel in its entirety may wish to call into question.

Unlike most literary criticism which has focused on aspects of homosexuality in Proust's novel, I shall not be addressing the issue of Proust's transposition of the sexes, nor his treatment and representation of specific homosexual characters.[3] Instead, with explicit reference to metaphor and language, I will dissect this long disquisition on the 'men–women of Sodom', in an attempt to delineate the ground being staked out by this reverse discourse. Does Proust's 'essay' signal a slippage between the medical and the literary in ways apposite to this book? Is it reverse discourse or camouflage? How is it that a homosexual man could reject the concept of homosexuality? What does it tell us about the nature of discourse, the subtle modes of its articulation, the limits of its meanings, and the politics of its use within the hegemonic order? Doesn't it suggest an inequality embedded in the very definition of homosexuality?

---

2   Marcel Proust, *A la recherche du temps perdu*, vol. 4: *Sodome et Gomorrhe* [1921], trans. Terence Kilmartin, Chatto & Windus, 1992. All page references will appear in the text, indicated by the abbreviation SG. All references to the earlier version, 'La race maudite', in *Contre Sainte-Beuve*, trans. Sylvia Townsend-Warner, Chatto & Windus, 1958, will appear in the text indicated by the abbreviation SB.

3   See, for example, Justin O'Brien, 'Albertine the Ambiguous: Notes on Proust's Transposition of the Sexes', *PMLA* 64 (1949), 933–52.

Marcel the Ambiguous

Gide called Proust "the great master of dissimulation", accusing him of "camouflage" and calling *Sodom and Gommorrah* "this offence against truth."[4] Proust told Gide that one can write about anything so long as one never uses 'I'; a tactic Gide, of course, thought unsuitable.[5] Gide, as stated in chapter one, disclaimed Proust's use of the Third Sex model, and Andre Maurois suggests we contrast Proust's book with Gide's to gain a fuller picture of inversion,[6] the two documents complementing one another.

Whereas Gide insisted on being open about his proclivities, Proust preferred to maintain an ambiguity around his. An interesting notion which Proust never actually incorporated into his novel reads:

> An author who writes about homosexuals with fairness owes it to himself never to share their pleasures, even if he considers them blameless. He is like a defrocked priest who once he has convinced people how absurd it is to impose celibacy upon the clergy, must remain chaste, so that he is not suspected of having been led into an indulgent moral position by personal interest rather than by love of the truth.[7]

We know from biographical data that Proust did "share their pleasures", so his disingenuity is telling. He clearly believed an openly homosexual writer to be the last person qualified to write fairly or truthfully about homosexuality, precisely because of their "personal interest". For this reason he made his narrator, Marcel, heterosexual, transposed the gender of his own lovers, and kept quiet about his homosexuality, making "love of the truth" his guiding light. Yet how far is such disingenuity compatible with a love of the truth?

---

[4] Gide, *Journals,* 2.109–10.
[5] Oscar Wilde offered Gide the same advice: Never use 'I'. See André Gide, *Oscar Wilde,* trans. Bernard Frechtman, William Kimber, 1951.
[6] Andre Maurois, *The Quest For Proust* [1949], trans. Gerard Hopkins, Penguin, 1950, 234.
[7] Cited in Antoine Compagnon, *Proust: Between Two Centuries,* trans. Richard E. Goodkin, Columbia University Press, 1992, 109.

Moreover, can we blame Proust for taking such a stand? David Halperin, writing in relation to the posthumous disclosure of Foucault's sadomasochistic activities and the ways in which this was used to discredit Foucault's position as an intellectual, justifies Proust's sentiments when he says: "to speak as a gay man about a topic that directly implicates one's own interests is already to surrender a sizable share of one's claims to be heard, listened to, and taken seriously."[8] In this light, it is easy to understand why Proust shied away from public disclosure; it would have instantly disqualified his writing in the eyes of a homophobic culture, as well as closing off invaluable sources of research essential for his novel. Indeed, much of the admiration and respect he received for his 'scientific and objective approach' was precisely because he was not known to be homosexual,[9] while much of the criticism of *Corydon* was precisely because Gide was known to be.

It's shocking to reflect that these procedures of objectification and subjection through which homophobic discourse works were no less dangerous for Foucault than for Proust and Gide over half a century earlier. It's still impossible in our culture for homosexuals to wrestle from the heterosexual hegemony the authority and right to the truth of their condition. The 'reality' of homosexuality is never the property of homosexuals themselves, but a cultural construction under whose reign they serve: in short, a discourse. Paradoxically – and non-sensically – one's contribution to this discourse is invalidated by one's involvement in it. As Halperin comments, "Anyone against whom biographical description can be so deployed in the first

---

8 Halperin, *Saint Foucault*, 138. It's disheartening to think that this is still the case.
9 Most critics praised Proust's treatment of inversion, and his psychological insight into the subject. Edmond Jaloux's response in *Le Bulletin de la maison du livres français*, 22 April 1922, is not untypical: "Several of his observations will obviously find a place among scientific studies, on the same footing as laboratory experiments" (cited in Leighton Hodson [ed.], *Marcel Proust and the Critical Heritage*, 149). Gide, however, was seen as having too vested an interest in the topic: "Proust has done more for the toleration of the outcast group than did Gide, who was a confessed member himself. A confession like Gide's arouses emotions, while a reasonable and sympathetic analysis like Proust's appeals to the heart through the intellect" (Milton Hindus, *The Proustian Vision*, Columbia University Press, 1954, 242).

place already lacks the requisite cultural authority to frustrate its deployment" (SF, 137).

Sexuality and the claims on it are an issue of private and public knowledge – who knows and what they do with such knowledge,[10] as well as know how much knowledge is acquired and circulated. The sustaining mechanism of such knowledge is discourse, and by it the category of the human sciences referred to by 'sexuality' obtains its meanings. The tension between Gide's position and that of Proust dramatizes the impossibility of homosexuals to speak for and about themselves in a homophobic culture. It also emphasizes what was at stake in reversing the discourse which subjugated homosexuals as objects of analysis and disavowed their existence as speaking subjects, whilst at the same time extracting their confessions to activate that objectification.

The initial concept of an outlet for Proust's views on homosexuality metamorphosed over a period of years from its humble beginnings as an idea for a magazine article into a short story[11] (which didn't appear in print until 1954) and finally into the opening chapter of one volume of a long novel, each manoeuvre further replacing any implied subjectivity with authorial and artistic objectivity. The 'knowing I' was not to be confused with the morally suspect 'knowledgeable I'. Any knowledge about homosexuality was to be seen as coming from observation rather than first-hand experience. Perhaps for this reason Proust adopted the most scientifically validated trope of same-sex desire: the Third Sex.

Proust believed that what he had to say was both original and psychologically true. In a letter to Gide he states that in the character of Charlus he "tried to portray the homosexual in love with virility because he is a Woman without realizing it [...] I by no means claim this to be the only type of homosexual. But

---

10 See Sedgwick, *Epistemology of the Closet*, 51–4.
11 Marcel Proust, *Selected Letters*, vol. 2: *1904–1909*, ed. Philip Kolb, trans. Terence Kilmartin, Collins, 1989, 371.

it is a very interesting kind and one which, I believe, has never been described."[12]

Never described in literature before, perhaps, but medical discourse had been deploying such ideas for several decades; ideas which had their origins in the pseudo-scientific, quasi-literary writings of a man who lacked any formal training in the natural sciences or medicine, and whose political programme was emancipatory: Karl Heinrich Ulrichs (1825–1895).[13]

Bodies That Natter

In a questionnaire Proust completed at the age of fifteen, he gave as "the quality I want to see in a man" as "Feminine charm", whilst his favourite quality in a woman was given as "the virtues of a man,"[14] testifying to a strong (and precocious) intellectual interest in androgyny, or trans-gender behaviour, a desire to subvert or challenge traditional gender values. The adult Proust remained intrigued by reversals of gender roles, and his novel contains numerous examples of 'masculine' women and 'feminine' men.[15]

It is perhaps not surprising, then, that he advocates in 'La race maudite' the popular scientific explanation of homosexuality as represented by the term third sex. Indeed, an early title for the essay was 'La race des tantes' ('The Race of Queens'). Barrere's *Argot and Slang Dictionary* (1889) gives 'queen' as a translation of the French word 'tante' (lit. 'aunt'), which we are told denotes a 'passive sodomist.'[16] In this fragment from Proust's unpublished notebooks he indicates what he saw as the signifying potency of the word *tante*:

---
12 Ibid., 2.374. Emphasis added. Interestingly, Gide was beginning work on *Corydon* around the same time.
13 See Hubert Kennedy, *Ulrichs: The Life & Works of Karl Heinrich Ulrichs, Pioneer of the Modern Gay Movement*, Alyson Publications, 1988.
14 Quoted in Philippe Michel-Thiriet, *The Book of Proust*, trans. Jan Dalley, Chatto & Windus, 1989, 59.
15 See Rivers, *Proust and the Art of Love*, 227–54, for a discussion of the role of androgyny in Proust's novel. For a discussion on the Third Sex, see Gert Hekman, '"A Female Soul In A Male Body": Sexual Inversion as Gender Inversion in Nineteenth Century Sexology', in Herdt (ed.), *Third Sex, Third Gender*, 222.
16 Quoted in Neil Bartlett, *Who Was That Man? A Present for Mr Oscar Wilde*, Serpent's Tail, 1988, 96.

This word would be particularly appropriate to the purpose of my book in which the characters to whom it is applicable, being almost all old and worldly, appear for the most part, in social gatherings where they strut and chatter, magnificently dressed and widely ridiculed. The *aunts*! The mere word conveys to us a vision of their solemnity and their get-up. The mere word wears skirts and brings to the eye a picture of the aunts pluming themselves in that fashionable setting, and twittering like birds in all the strangeness of a different species.[17]

While he denied that this was "the only type of homosexual,"[18] it is the only type with which he wants to deal. Proust is completely enamoured with the richly evocative powers of the word as a signifier for the homosexual man, but his enthusiasm belies his phobic intentions. In a letter to Gide, Proust gleefully relishes the idea that, in Gide's novel *Les caves du Vatican,* all Lafcadio's uncles are really aunts. He wants the metaphor to stand as a synonym for a secret, shared knowledge.[19]

Every last drop of misogyny implicit in this image of twittering, vain, and, perhaps most significantly, sexless womanhood could be seen to be imported into the usage of such a resonant phrase to describe a certain male homosexual, except that great affection is displayed for Marcel's real aunts throughout *A la recherche*. Proust clearly didn't consider tante to be a term of abuse or insult, but rather, a term of affection, even a compliment. As Sedgwick has pointed out, rather than having an inevitable and indisputable link with passive sodomy, the performance of actual, specific sexual behaviours is effectively excised from such an epithet, which can be applied to "any man who displays a queenly demeanor, whatever he may do with other men in bed." Tantes are merely bodies that natter, nothing more, their behaviour indicative of a femininity not contingent on sexual activity (or, rather, passivity). "Furthermore", Sedgwick writes:

---

[17] Quoted in Maurois, *The Quest For Proust,* 223–4.
[18] Marcel Proust, *Selected Letters,* vol. 3: *1910–17,* ed. P. Kolb, trans. Terence Kilmartin, Harper Collins, 1992, 268.
[19] Ibid., 3.248.

'aunt', used about a man, alludes to a gender-transitive persona which, however, it doesn't particularly pretend to stabilize in the dyadic terms of gender inversion: the 'aunt' usage long predates and surely influences, but is not adequated by, the rationalized discursive production of the invert.[20]

In other words, queens/*tantes* were calling each other queens/tantes long before science discursively constructed the homosexual along an axis of effeminacy, or queeniness, suggesting that what science succeeded in doing, to enormous and far-reaching effect, was to establish such behaviour as an essential, identity-fixing denominator in the formation of a gender-inverted body, rather than allowing it to exist as a potent and direct challenge to normativizing concepts of gender stability. This belief in the homosexual's innate femininity led Proust to prefer the term 'inversion' to 'homosexuality'.[21]

What's in a Name?

Compagnon sees Proust's rejection of the term homosexuality as a shift away from the medical establishment,[22] despite the fact that he used instead the term inversion which was the more popular term in France at that time. Yet Proust's preference for the term invert derives from its association with femininity, and has nothing to do with distancing himself from the medical establishment. Indeed, the word invert stems from sexual inver-

---

20 Sedgwick, 'Tales of the Avunculate', 59.

21 Compagnon claims that Proust's most radical contribution to the scientific discourse on homosexuality is his insistence on the hereditary transference of femininity in cases of inversion from female relatives to their male homosexual offspring. There is no elaboration of the exact radicalness of this doctrine, which appears to be a straightforward adoption of Ulrichs' ideas. Compagnon, *Proust*, 247. Proust powerfully evokes the Degeneration theories so popular in the 1890s. Indeed, despite Pierre-Quint's claim that Proust's account is more contemporary than Gide's (see Eva Ahlstedt, *André Gide et le débat sur l'homosexualité*, Acta Universitatis Gothoburgensis, 1994, 74), it would be more accurate to say, as Compagnon does, that "Proust's notions belong to the end of the nineteenth century and are an anachronism by the time the novel is published" (Compagnon, *Proust*, 241). It's worth remembering here that the encounter between Charlus and Jupien occurs, within, the chronology of the novel, in 1899, and is therefore not contemporaneous with its publication in 1921, but with the medical theories articulated within Proust's 'essay'.

22 Compagnon, *Proust*, 246.

sion, a term coined by Westphal, and could therefore be said to have much more scientific association than 'homosexual', which was coined by a novelist, Benkert.

Proust makes a clear distinction between the two words:

> Indeed, there is a slight difference. Homosexuals take great pride in not being inverts. According to the theory I am sketching out here – however fragmentary it might be – there are in fact no such things as homosexuals. However masculine the appearance of a fairy might be, his feelings of attraction to virile men come from an underlying femininity, although it may be hidden. If this is true, a homosexual is what an invert claims to be, what an invert believes himself in all good faith to be.[23]

There are no such things as homosexuals. There is no such thing as a desire for the same because the homosexual's desire for other men stems from an 'underlying femininity', which, however much he tries to hide it, is always there, threatening to break out, the motor behind his desire.

The reasons for Proust's dissatisfaction with the term homosexual and preference for invert may be clarified somewhat if we consider that the two terms were by no means interchangeable in late nineteenth century discourse; far from being synonyms, as pointed out in recent work by Chauncey, Halperin and Sedgwick. While homosexuality merely pinpointed same-sex activity, sexual inversion implied a reversal of gender roles, and was therefore much more appealing to Proust for describing his *hommes–femmes*.[24] The sexual unions envisaged by Proust between an invert and a virile man are, for him, clearly not examples of *homo*sexuality, a term he describes as "inept" (SG, 8). By constructing a psychic matrix in which feminine men desire masculine men, he is reinstating a fundamental heterosexuality to these acts between people of the same anatomical sex. For

---
23 *Ibid.*
24 For a brief outline of these differences and their historical implications see Segwick, *Epistemology of the Closet*, 157–59.

him the homosexual is always an invert and therefore always in a very real sense a woman. He claims, furthermore, that it is the invert's innate femininity that causes the homosexual man to idealize and desire manliness (SG, 17).

Proust maintains that homosexuals are invested with "the physical and moral characteristics of a race, sometimes beautiful, often hideous" (SG, 19). The deployment of such value-laden adjectives as 'beautiful' and 'hideous' threatens to disintegrate the notion of scientific objectivity the text strives to maintain. We are told that homosexuals resemble other (i.e. real) men "in appearance only" (SG, 17), suggesting that it is the interior, the soul, that is the seat of this femininity from which his desire for men emanates, placing Proust's views in line with those of Ulrichs.

But, as with Ulrichs, a major, irreconcilable contradiction arises from this theory. For if homosexual men bear "the physiognomy of a nation", if they quite literally constitute a separate sex, race, or species with its own set of characteristics, how can they simultaneously resemble other men? Proust has trapped himself between what Sedgwick has termed the minoritizing and universalizing views of same-sex desire. The former regards homosexuality as "an issue of active importance primarily for a small, distinct, relatively fixed homosexual minority", whilst the latter sees it as "an issue of continuing, determinative importance in the lives of people across the spectrum of sexualities".[25]

According to Proust, the majority of homosexuals shun one another to avoid detection, concealing and denying that they belong to a race "the name of which is the vilest of insults" (SG, 19). "They hate and pour scorn on others of their race, and never go near them" (SG, 167). In each other they merely inspire "the chagrin of discovering in their own bosoms the warning that the thing they believe to be a natural love is a sickly madness – as well as that womanliness which offends them" (SB, 161) That

---

25 Ibid., 1. Proust is clearly unaware of this contradictory aspect of his theory, for he rigidly maintains throught his essay these antithetical ideas of homosexual men as a third sex and homosexual behaviour as something which can go undetected for years.

womanliness is described in the most phobic way by Proust, for whom, in *tantes*,

> The woman is almost half-declared. Her breasts emerge from them, they seize every opportunity of fancy dress to show them off, they are as fond of dancing and dress and cosmetics as girls are, and at the most sedate gatherings break into giggling fits, or start singing. (SB, 165)

It is difficult to take such writing seriously now that this stereotype has been deconstructed and seen for what it is. But it exemplifies the way in which a particular trope conveyed discursive meaning at a time when homosexuality had little political visibility. The field of visibility was dominated by this trope and its power to signify the cultural concept of homosexuality far outweighed its bearing on reality, which leads us to ask not simply how this trope came to dominate the visual field, but also why? The cultural significance and political function of the third sex trope is suggested by one line in 'La race maudite' – a line taken from a poem by Vigny: "The two sexes shall die, each in a place apart!" (SG, 18). This explicit reference to the polarization of the two sexes within a discourse on the third sex foregrounds sexual dimorphism whilst at the same time creating a discursive space *outside* of it for the existence of a third sex as an 'excluded middle'. Whilst this third sex is contingent upon the existence of the other two, it acts not as a bridge between them but as a wall, reinforcing the polarities in social roles and sexual behaviours. As Trumbach has argued, "in the majority of human beings, only women [desire] men. The condition of the effeminate sodomite emphasized that most men did not".[26] The third sex, therefore, functioned as a scapegoat for what Sedgwick calls homosexual panic in a culture that disavowed the existence of an amorphous, non-object specific human sexuality.[27] It made available

---
26 Randolph Trumbach, 'Gender and the Homosexual Role in Modern Western Culture: The Eighteenth and Nineteenth Centuries Compared', in *Homosexuality Which Homosexuality?*, GMP, 1989, 153.
27 On homosexual panic see Sedgwick, *Epistemology of the Closet*, 19–20; 182–7; and *Between Men*, 83–96.

a visible, discursively inscribed portrait of the kind of man who desired other men, with the result that men who wished to avoid the social stigma attached to such behaviour need only avoid appearing to belong to such a minority by avoiding any form of effeminacy. It was a policing of gender identity much more than it was a policing of sexual activity. Trumbach writes: "Human biology was now supposed to be so structured that the majority of persons did not know what it was like to desire persons of the same gender."[28] And the minority who did know were just that: a minority, a race apart, a third sex whose function was to ensure the maintenance of a dyadic gender system; a socially marginalized but culturally central imago of the homosexual male: what Jeffrey Weeks describes as a labeling process "of the most explicit kind, drawing an impassable border between acceptable and abhorrent behaviour".[29]

Hideous Visibilities
With enormous subtlety and finesse, Proust's narrator slips in the occasional line which undermines the dominant theme of disgust and disease which dominates the text. For example, homosexuals are described as "a reprobate section of the human collectivity but *an important one*" (SG, 20, emphasis added). In what way important? Could Proust be hinting at what Lynn Segal explicitly pinpoints when she writes that "the maintenance and stability of contemporary heterosexual masculinity is deeply dependent upon its distance from, and obsessive denunciation of, an opposing category – that of the homosexual"[30]?

This distance is achieved by constructing the homosexual as a race apart, a race so distinct from so-called normal men that there can be no confusion between the two. The denunciation Segal mentions is articulated, primarily, through violence, both discursive and physical. Within the terms of this double bind, homosexual man is an oxymoron, a contradiction. The

---

[28] Trumbach, 'Gender and the Homosexual Role in Modern Western Culture', 161.
[29] Jeffrey Weeks, *Coming Out: Homosexual Politics in Britain from the Nineteenth Century to the Present*, Quartet, 1977, 21.
[30] Lynn Segal, *Slow Motion: Changing Masculinities Changing Men*, Virago, 1990, 137.

constitution in our culture of desire, sexuality and gender along separate axes of interpretation allows for a crossing-point where we might locate the figure of the Third Sex. Marjorie Garber acknowledges the disruptive potential of a third term to the fixity of binary thought:

> The 'third' is that which questions binary thinking and introduces a crisis [...].But what is crucial here – and I can hardly underscore this strongly enough – is that the 'third term' is not a term. Much less is it a sex, certainly not an instantiated 'blurred' sex as signified by a term like 'androgyne' or 'hermaphrodite', although these words have culturally specific significance at certain historical moments. The 'third' is a mode of articulation, a way of describing a space of possibility.[31]

Garber refutes the notion of a third sex because it's too easy and fails to disrupt the primacy of the other two sexes. For her the third term is "something that challenges the possibility of harmonious and stable binary symmetry". Within the Western gender system, however, the male/female binary is hardly one of symmetry, but rather dissymmetry. Likewise, Proust refers to the 'perfect symmetry' between Jupien's movements and those of Charlus (SG, 5), although, again, dissymmetry is more apparent. As Laqueur has shown, the two sex model is of relatively recent invention,[32] and if women are the second sex, then homosexuals come in at third place, a warning against blurring the gender boundaries. The invention of homosexuality as representative of a third sex is contemporaneous with the implementation of the two sex model. Garber is right, there is no third sex, but there is a cultural third term in the field of sexuality and gender represented by homosexuality.

---

31 Marjorie Garber, *Vested Interests: Cross-Dressing and Cultural Anxiety*, Penguin, 1992, 11.
32 Thomas Laqueur, *Making Sex: Body and Gender from the Greeks to Freud*, Harvard University Press, 1990.

Through such gestures as 'a hysterical spasm', or 'a shrill laugh', the homosexual can be rendered 'hideously visible' (SG, 23), making him look "no more like the common run of men than those apes with melancholy ringed eyes and prehensile feet who dress up in dinner-jackets and black ties" (SG, 23). For Proust, the effeminate homosexual is quite explicitly presented as a figure of fun, a ridiculous creature who, by virtue of being so visibly homosexual, is perceived by his (non-effeminate) fellow inverts as a "compromising associate", and by society as an unacceptable threat to the maintenance of stable gender roles, even as it shores them up. In the *Contre Saint-Beuve* version, effeminate homosexuals are described as the "dregs of their race, the braceletted sect", from whom non-effeminate homosexuals recoil as if from "some intolerable stink" (SB, 168). Strong words of disgust. Quite clearly, it is not sexual acts so much as gender performances that are being subjected to such heavy policing.

The ape simile provides, however paradoxically, a useful example of gender as performative, masculinity as an aping – and reinscription – of certain gestures associated with the socially constructed figure of that gendered category: man. Rather than being the natural expression of an innate and fixed gender core, these gestures generate the very identity from which they are understood to originate. As Judith Butler writes, "there is no gender identity behind the expressions of gender; that identity is performatively constituted by the very 'expressions' that are said to be its results".[33] Likewise, Proust seems to be saying that masculine and feminine behaviours are not so much the inevitable results of a pre-social or 'natural' sexual identity, but rather the socially contingent marks of gender.[34] Effeminacy is the signifier

---

33 Butler, *Gender Trouble*, 25.
34 This seems to me a much more satisfactory explanation of Proust's fascination with androgyny than that offered by Rivers, who resorts to Aristophanes' tale in the *Symposium* of an origin human race consisting of three forms: male–female, male–male, and female–female. Since Zeus split them down the middle to weaken them, they have forever been in search of their original 'other half'; hence heterosexuality, homosexuality and lesbianism. Rivers writes, "Sodom corresponds to Aristophanes' divided and dispersed male body, and Gomorrah to Aristophanes' divided and dispersed female body. And love, in both accounts, is an attempt to reunify what once was whole" (Riv-

of the 'woman within',³⁵ only ever connoting a (passive) homosexual identity. In this way, homosexuality itself emerges as a third gender, a performative category construed as the consequence of a core femininity while in truth being "constituted by the very 'expressions' that are said to be its results." Butler's analysis offers an insight into the workings of the third sex/inversion trope which has haunted same-sex desire for over a century. An identity, an essence, an interiority has been constructed as the foundation for and cause of particular sexual expressions, when in fact the identity is constructed by those particular sexual acts, not *vice versa*. There are only homosexual acts. The surface has been read as depth, when in fact it is only surface. Proust foregrounds the aesthetics of homosexual behaviour, placing great emphasis on the surface, on what is visible, even if he reads this surface as indicative of a depth characterized by an innate femininity. Through analogies with the virtual impossibility of fertilization in certain botanical species, the narrator establishes a strong link between homosexual congress and the procreative imperative in nature.³⁶

It Takes One to Know One

Nature plays a complex and curious role in Proust's theory. A lacunae in the 1909 version is filled by its translator, Sylvia Townsend Warner, with an evocative phrase which echoes Krafft-Ebing, who described the homosexual as "the stepchild of Nature." Proust calls the homosexual "this being towards whom nature was so [and here Warner inserts: step-motherly]" (SB, 164). Warner offers no explanation for this very plausible choice of adjective to describe the relationship between homo-

---

ers, *Proust and the Art of Love*, 224). His account forecloses the possibility of seeing in Proust's cross-gendering a critique of the dimorphic gender system.
35 Mario Miele, *Homosexuality and Liberation: Elements of a Gay Critique* [1977], trans. David Fernbach, GMP, 1980, 31. Miele maintains that homosexuality and femininity are linked.
36 In the 1909 version in *Contre Saint-Beuve*, Proust argues that, societal persecution notwithstanding, homosexuals would face enormous difficulties finding partners due to their scarcity (SB, 164). This contradicts the later version, in which he claims "these exceptional creatures with whom we commiserate are a vast crowd […] and commiserate themselves for being too many rather than too few" (SG, 36).

sexuality and nature. Yet, as with Krafft-Ebing's phrase, this explicitly places the homosexual outside the traditional zone of nature – not nature's direct offspring – whilst at the same time acknowledging a tortuous and indirect lineage between the two. Mother Nature is usurped by Step-mother Nature and the progenitive link is displaced.

Culturally, the figure of the stepmother is characterized by cruelty and sadism, as in the fairytale of Cinderella.[37] But Proust's nature would seem to be both "fiendish and beneficent" (SG, 53), playing the trick of inversion whilst at the same time furnishing the invert with a sixth sense enabling him to recognize those beings with whom he can achieve union, as witnessed in the pick-up between Charlus and Jupien. In other words, it takes one to know one.[38]

Proust's narrator, Marcel, credits homosexuality with beauty and harmony and importance. Proust's fascination with sexual duality directs him to examples of hermaphrodism in natural history. What the hermaphroditic organism is in the animal kingdom, the third sex is in humans. When he talks of an "initial hermaphroditism of which certain rudiments of male organs in the anatomy of women and female organs in that of men seem still to preserve a trace", it is a biological rather than a mythological originality to which he is referring: an originality that predates "the age of Greece" (SG, 34–35). Any resistance to the sickness model must be located here, where his usage of words such as "miracle", "marvelous", "beauty" and "harmony"

---

[37] This contrasts strongly with the figure of the *aunt*, which is maternal and caring. Both, however, are symbolically childless, or at least signify a non-procreative relation.

[38] Whilst nature clearly provides signs and ways of reading them, Proust also sites examples of groups of homosexual men socializing in a café and casting yearning glances at the young 'lions' at a neighbouring table, only to discover years later, by which time the young men have become stout and grizzled Charluses, that they too were homosexual, but with a different set of codes, "other external symbols" (SG, 22) unrecognizable by those from another clique. What's interesting here is the juxtaposition of nature and culture. The homosexual, whom one would imagine possessed of experiential knowledge of the superficiality of 'true nature', is seen here accepting the behaviour of others as indicative of an essential self: the young men's bragging about mistresses is taken at face value, when we have already been told that nature has ways of rendering homosexuals recognizable to one another. Nature is here duped by culture. Proust seems to be enjoying contradicting the commonism of 'it takes one to know one' which he has already established as in some sense true.

(SG, 32–3) encourages the reader to alter their perception of this accursed race; where, despite its inevitable sterility, sex between men is seen as having its place within nature rather than outside it; a place the importance of which is only discernable once instinctive aversion has been cast aside:

> When I followed my instinct only, the jellyfish used to revolt me at Balbec; but if I had the eyes to regard them, like Michelet, from the standpoint of natural history and aesthetics, I saw an exquisite blue girandole. (SG, 31)

The narrator seems to be suggesting a radical conjoining of natural history with aesthetics when viewing homosexuality too; only then can the true significance and exquisite natural beauty of such a phenomenon be appreciated. Aesthetics, arts-for-arts'-sake, would not only remove the need for moral judgement, but would in fact suggest a positive amorality. If nature provides inverts with the propensity to seek out sexual partners, we must therefore acknowledge their rightful place in the natural order: a conjunction the miraculous possibility of which is as providential as the bee ("a very rare insect") fertilizing the orchid ("a captive flower"). But more than this, we must eradicate moral judgement and observe from a purely aesthetic perspective if we are to proceed beyond an initial (and, he suggests are, inevitable) revulsion. This is a radical insertion of the aesthetic into the naturalistic, and, like Wilde before him, Proust would seem to favour the aesthetic over the naturalistic as a standpoint from which to view any action or behaviour. Unlike Gide, who saw the haphazardness of nature as occasioning same-sex behaviour almost as a by-product of the pursuit of pleasure, Proust sees a very precise order to nature; an order which facilitates the satisfaction of homosexual desire by something he considers nothing short of a miracle. But a miracle the very occurrence of which signals a biological intention.

The pick-up between Jupien and Charlus, for example, is described as "not, however, positively comic, it was stamped with a strangeness, or if you like a naturalness, the beauty of which steadily increased" (SG, 5). Not only does this foreground the ocular, the aesthetics of the scene, but, as Sedgwick points out, it equates strangeness with naturalness. Moreover,

> To let *l'étrangeté* equal *le naturel* [...] is not simply to equate opposites but to collapse a domino chain of pairings, each with its different, historical gay involvements: natural/un-natural, natural/artifical, habitual/de-familiarized, common/rare, native/foreign.[39]

For the strange to be natural, or the natural to be strange, is to confuse existing categories and the ways in which we make sense of the world. This inversion of meanings is Proust's biggest challenge to taxonomics, for, much more than Gide's polemics, it stakes out a place in nature for the strange and a beauty for those things commonly perceived as hideous. He avoids the question of morality by addressing the question of aesthetics, a field in which the strange and natural beauty of homosexuality has a value.

The Symbolic Behind

Despite his emphasis on the beauty of homosexuality, Proust was well aware that *Sodome & Gomorrhe* would offend homosexuals with its negative insistence on sickness and effeminacy, but he seemed unconcerned. In a letter to Natalie Barney, he states almost proudly: "My sodomites are all horrible."[40] According to Gide, Proust confessed to having put all the "attractive, affectionate and charming elements contained in his homosexual recollections" into the heterosexual characters of his novel, a move which left him only the "grotesque and the abject" for the homosexual ones.[41] This suggests a deliberate decision to avoid any attractive representation of same-sex relationships, a conscious refusal to challenge the dominant fiction. Certainly,

---

39 Sedgwick, *Epistemology of the Closet*, 229.
40 Quoted in George Painter, *Proust: A Biography*, 2 vols., Chatto & Windus, 1959, 329. Reprinted by Pimlico, 1996.
41 Gide, *Journals*, 2.267

"Proust knew personally some of the men who developed the idea that homosexuality was a congenital pathology."[42] Could this explain why he preferred the sickness model? As Rivers states, "The idea of a guilt-free, nonpathological homosexuality was available to Proust, had he chosen to take advantage of it."[43] But the fact is, he didn't. Perhaps his own ill-health predisposed him to find in the sickness model a sense of self-justification, rendering the figure of the homosexual as sick and psychologically crippled actually attractive to him. Gide suggests this: "What we consider vile, an object of laughter and disgust, does not seem so repulsive to [Proust]."[44] Or was he augmenting a political programme which can be subsequently traced through writers such as Genet and Dennis Cooper to the recent celebration of perversity under the banner of Queer? What we might call celebrating abjection. This would certainly allow us to map the disparity between Gide and Proust onto the current antagonism between the old school gay movement and the nascent queer movement. Gide's insistence on the naturalness of homo-love contradicts Proust's avowal and celebration of its perversity in much the same way. Proust was clearly seduced by the notion of sickness abetting genius and raised his own suffering to the level of martyrdom. Towards the end of his life, as he worked on the novel despite doctor's warnings to rest, he seems to be actively seeking death through the redemption of his art.[45] There is a definite sense in him of how death drives life.[46]

Throughout his childhood and early adulthood, illness had been a mode of communication between Proust and his mother, a way of wrestling her affections away from his brother. As an older man, as he battled for breath to correct galley proofs, there is a strong sense that not simply illness, but creative genius through illness, has become the dying writer's *raison d'être*. Given Proust's belief in the creative potential, even superiority, of ill-

---

[42] David F. Greenberg, *The Construction of Homosexuality*, University of Chicago Press, 1988, 418.
[43] Rivers, *Proust and the Art of Love*, 166.
[44] Gide, *Journals*, 2.216.
[45] See Leo Bersani, *The Culture of Redemption*, Harvard University Press, 1990.
[46] See Jonathan Dollimore, 'Death and the Self', unpublished paper, 1996.

ness, it was perhaps inevitable that he would reject the notion of healthy uranism promoted by Gide. For Proust, the taint of femininity was one that discoloured all members of the accursed race, whereas for Gide there was some hope in those who had managed to avoid such a taint. In Proust's model, therefore, there is no such thing as homosexuality, only inversion, the result of an atavistic femininity which positioned male homosexuals in a feminine paradigm; indeed, made of them (symbolic) women.

Silverman's reading of the femininity trope in Proust as a challenge to phallic primacy is enacted through seeing the primary erotic modality in the novel as lesbianism.[47] Certainly, there is a strong sense in which the Phallus loses importance in the Proustian libidinal economy. But this is achieved mainly through a symbolic castration of the invert: "the unconscious visible woman in him seeks the masculine organ" (SG, 25). There is never any sense of a male desire for a male. Even an invert "so enamoured of, who so prided himself upon, his virility, to whom all other men seemed odiously effeminate" such as Charlus is a woman (SG, 4), because in Proust's world it is desire for men which feminizes. Even if Charlus plays the 'male' role with Jupien, such positionality is no antidote against an all-pervasive feminization. For if desire is lack and you desire men, then maleness must be what you lack, and having sex with other men is a ceaselessly repetitive quest to acquire it, whether you are a top or a bottom.

Whether Charlus is a top with all his partners we don't know, obviously, but his backside is certainly a salient feature and crude synecdoche throughout the novel. Jupien comments: "What a big bum you have!" (SG, 11),whilst elsewhere he is described as having an "almost symbolic behind" (SG, 890). For the homosexual, the behind will always be symbolic, in a way, as a site of both pleasure and anxiety, whether he takes pleasure there or not, because the assumption will always be that he does. When Marcel overhears Jupien and Charlus having anal sex, he thinks that a murder is taking place, and concludes "that there is

---

47 Kaja Silverman, *Male Subjectivity at the Margins*, Routledge, 1992.

another thing as noisy as pain, namely pleasure, especially when there is added to it – in the absence of fear of pregnancy which could not be the case here… – an immediate concern about cleanliness" (SG, 10).

This concern with cleanliness is something about which Freud also wrote: "The excremental is all too intimately and inseparably bound up with the sexual; the position of the genitals – *inter urinas et faeces* – remains the decisive and unchangeable factor."[48] In *Three Essays on Sexuality*, however, he dismisses this disgust as purely conventional:

> I hope I shall not be accused of partisanship when I assert that people who try to account for this disgust by saying that the organ in question serves the function of excretion and comes in contact with excrement […] are not much more to the point than hysterical girls who account for their disgust at the male genital by saying that it serves to void urine.[49]

The reference to hysterical girls makes us wince, but for the rest, it's almost revolutionary. Interesting, too, how Freud is concerned, like Proust, not to be seen as sharing the pleasures referred to. Scientific knowledge must be based on observation alone, not participation (see chapter four).

More recently, Richard Davenport-Hines has written about the added anxiety over anal sex since AIDS, and the way in which the virus is presented in the media as punishment on homosexuals for "abusing their arses". He writes:

> Objectively the discrimination between penises and rectums is nonsense; given the greater horror that shit commands over urine in our culture, the distinction is understandable;

---

48 Sigmund Freud, *Standard Edition of the Complete Works*, trans. James Strachey, Hogarth Press, 1964, 2.189.
49 Sigmund Freud, 'Three Essays on Sexuality', in *The Pelican Freud Library*, vol. 7, ed. Angela Richards, Penguin, 1974–86.

but nonsense is still nonsense, whether acculturated, atavistic or adopted as an excuse for journalistic bullying.[50]

Proust relates the fear of cleanliness conversely to a fear of pregnancy, suggesting that all sexual intercourse has its anxieties, just as pleasure is akin to pain. The anxieties for the passive homosexual are intimately linked with the threat of emasculation and feminization – a feminization culturally encoded into the act of receptivity itself. By insisting that such feminization is attached also to the active partner, Proust goes some way to deconstructing the violent hierarchy of the active/passive binarism; yet he does so at the risk of colluding with the dominant fiction which perceives homosexuality as always and necessarily opposed to what it means to be male. As such, Proust ultimately reinforces the normative scientific assumption that male homosexual desire is never anything other than an expression of an essential femininity, a belief which has been the basis of both homophobic and homosexual discourses in this century.

---

50 Richard Davenport-Hines, *Sex, Death and Punishment: Attitudes to Sex and Sexuality in Britain Since the Renaissance*, Fontana Press, 1991, 336.

Chapter Three

Beautiful Flowers and Perverse Ruins:
Edward Carpenter's Intermediate Sex

> *Nature, it might appear, in mixing the elements*
> *Which go to compose each individual,*
> *Does not always keep her two groups of*
> *Ingredients – which represent the two sexes –*
> *Properly apart, but often throws them*
> *Crosswise in a somewhat baffling manner.*
> – Edward Carpenter

Edward Carpenter (1844–1929) has long been regarded as a pioneer of same-sex desire, his championing of Whitman's notion of comradeship seen as progressive and important in the development of a gay identity and history.[1] Yet if we look more closely at what Carpenter was saying it becomes apparent that he never condoned sexual relationships between homosexuals; rather, he flatly denied the importance of sex and promoted instead the spiritual and creative aspects of same-sex love, painting a rather anodine and sexless picture of brotherly affection that is far removed from reality and could be said to have actually distorted the truth of homosexuality as a specifically *sexual* identity. A close reading of Carpenter's *The Intermediate Sex* (1908) reveals his theory as having more in common with homo*sociality* than homo*sexuality*, and therefore highlights once again the absence of a relevant, unprejudiced theory of same-sex *desire*.

What is radical, however, is Carpenter's insistence on the important role played by homosexuals in the production of cul-

---

[1] See Noel Grieg's Introduction to Carpenter: *Selected Writings* 1; Sheila Rowbotham and Jeffrey Weeks, *Socialism and the New Life: The Personal and Sexual Politics of Edward Carpenter and Havelock Ellis*, Pluto, 1977; Chuschichi Tsuzuki, *Edward Carpenter 1844–1929: Prophet of Human Fellowship*, Cambridge University Press, 1990; Jeffrey Weeks, *Coming Out: Homosexual Politics in Britain, from the Nineteenth Century to the Present*, Quartet, 1977, chapter 6; Ian Young, *The Stonewall Experiment*, Cassell, 1995, 30–5.

ture and art by virtue of their non-procreation, an idea I shall explore later in this chapter for its usefulness to this study. Lack of children is undoubtedly seen as one of the major differences between heterosexuals and homosexuals (albeit a recent one, given that prior to the development of a gay lifestyle, many homosexuals married and had children[2]) and may have some bearing on homosexual creativity if we accept that the creative urge is a universal one. As such, homosexual's non-procreation can be said to be of vital importance for the birth of ideas, of art, indeed of culture itself.

Literature vs. Science

Carpenter regarded homosexuality as a *new* phenomenon to be studied, categorized and understood, whilst also acknowledging that homosexual love – or comrade love – had been an important aspect of ancient Greek culture. One way of explaining this apparent contradiction is that, like Gide, Carpenter turned to history as a way of justifying homosexuality. The problem with this is that the past does not always or necessarily aid an understanding of the present. It's important to remember that Carpenter was writing at a historical juncture between a history in which homosexuality did not exist and a future in which it would become a diacritical marker of ontology. His comprehension of his own same-sex desires found resonance – as it did for many homosexual men – in ancient Greek culture, where love between men was often encouraged in armies, for example, on the understanding that a soldier would fight all the more ferociously if he was defending a lover.[3] At the same time, the new science of sexol-

---

[2] Until fairly recently, social pressures meant that many lesbians and gay men would have married and had children instead of leading open lives with members of their own sex. Oscar Wilde is a case in point. Having children did not, for him, constitute a sublimation of creative energies. He still produced art. Obviously, the argument runs the risk of being reductive if not seen in its entire complexity.

[3] Carpenter's 1914 text, *Intermediate Types among Primitive Folk*, explicitly states a belief in Uranians' ability at militarism (see *Selected Writings*, 1.248). Ironically, gay activist Peter Tatchell employed Carpenter's theories to support his arguments about gays in the military, suggesting that homosexual men should not want to collude with such a violent and patriarchal institution (*We Don't Want to March Straight: Masculinity, Gays and the Military*, Cassell, 1995, 49–50). Tatchell ignores the fact that Carpenter thought homosexuals make very good soldiers.

ogy offered men like Carpenter a way of theorizing their desires within the rubric of nature, albeit as (in Krafft-Ebing's phrase), 'step-children of nature'. In this sense, the 'homosexual' was indeed something new to be analysed and understood, although male–male love remained a transhistorical phenomenon.[4]

On the publication of his pamphlet *Homogenic Love and its Place in a Free Society* in 1895, Carpenter received a letter of praise from Horatio Brown, commending the "cool, quiet, convincing, scientific way" that Carpenter had treated "this difficult and, at present, obscure problem". There appears to have been no question hanging over Carpenter's assumption of scientific authority. Furthermore, the obscurity of the problem is seen as only capable of being clarified by such a scientific approach. Brown expressed concern at the possibility that the issue may remain the exclusive domain of *belles lettres*, insisting that "Doctors and Lawyers must be induced to take off their spectacles and look."[5]

Brown's letter dramatizes the fact that at the turn of the century, many people of the educated classes strongly believed that medicine could achieve what literature could not. Namely, an intelligent and dispassionate analysis of male–male love, devoid of both homophobic vitriol and flamboyant proselytism; an analysis which would educate and liberate, transforming social and judicial prejudice. That it was homosexual men of letters such as Carpenter and Addington Symonds, rather than men of

---

4 Significant debates abound concerning the exact date of birth of the homosexual. Constructionists like Foucault and Weeks pinpoint the late nineteenth century; others, such as Alan Bray, Rictor Norton and Randolph Trumbach put the date much earlier, in the 1700s, while John Boswell challenges such claims by using the term transhistorically. See John Boswell, *Christianity, Social Tolerance, and Homosexuality: Gay People in Western Europe from the Beginning of the Christian Era to the Fourteenth Century*, University of Chicago Press, 1980; Alan Bray, *Homosexuality in Renaissance England*, Gay Men's Press, 1982; Foucault, *The History of Sexuality*; Rictor Norton, *Mother Clap's Molly House*, Gay Men's Press, 1992; Randolph Trumbach, 'London's Sodomites: Homosexual Behaviour and Western Culture in the Eighteenth Century', *Journal of Social History* 11 (1977), 1–33; Weeks, *Coming Out*.

5 Quoted in Timothy D'Arch Smith, *Love in Earnest: Some Notes on the Lives and Writings of English 'Uranian' Poets 1889–1930*, Routledge & Kegan Paul, 1970, 20–1. The metaphor's implication is confusing: without their glasses, wouldn't the doctors and laywers be unable to see clearly? But at the same time, it establishes the homosexual body as a spectacle for the ever-vigilant medico-legal gaze.

science, who took up this challenge, under the guise of objective scientific study, directs me to two conclusions:

1. *Discursive symbiosis*. The discursive fields of literature and medicine were far less mutually exclusive as intellectual practices a century ago than they are now, allowing for traffic between the two areas of study almost unheard of today. This discursive symbiosis not only allowed men of science like Havelock Ellis, Max Nordau and Freud to write on literature and art, it also allowed men of letters and poets, such as Carpenter and Addington Symonds to engage with medicine, employing the medical terminology without being seen as lacking the qualifications or authority to work in that field. The economic drive to establish medicine as an exclusive epistemological field was in part fuelled by a desire to eradicate such interdisciplinary hybridization. Henceforth, medicine was promoted as a field of expertise and esoteric knowledge incomprehensible to the layperson. Herein lies the authoritarian power of the doctor, a vessel of knowledge to which we in the West invariably defer in matters concerning our own bodies, our own lives. In our century, Literature/Science has become a binarism as insurmountable as Hetero/Homo.

2. *Literary influence*. The transmission of ideas – the influence – from literature to medicine remains, on the whole, unrecognized, particularly by medicine. (Recall that the word homosexual was coined by a novelist[6] [see introduction]). Richard von Krafft-Ebing, the German-Austrian psychiatrist whose *Psychopathia Sexualis* (1886) was the Ur-text of sexology, wrote to Ulrichs stating that "It was the knowledge of your writings alone that induced me to the study of this highly important field."[7] Ulrichs was not a doctor. Were there no homosexual doctors, men who had read the likes of Ul-

---

6 See Silverstolpe, 'Benkert Was Not a Doctor'.
7 Kennedy, *Ulrichs*, 71. For a detailed account of Krafft-Ebing's role in the emergence of the homosexual, see Harry Oosterhuis, 'Richard von Krafft-Ebing's "Step-Children of Nature": Psychiatry and the Making of Homosexual Identity', in Vernon A. Rosario, *Science and Homosexualities*, Routledge, 1997, 67–88.

richs, Hirschfeld, Westphal *et al.*? In a very real sense, then, the 'homosexual was a fictional character.[8]

The invention of the homosexual in nineteenth century medical discourse was aided by the exigencies of homosexual self-invention, sexology being greatly dependent on homosexual *self*-disclosure. Books like *Psychopathia Sexualis* and *Sexual Inversion* consisted in the main of case histories. In a field reliant on the case history, doctors ingeniously got homosexuals to do their work for them. Homosexuals had no more more interest in science than they did in the opposite sex. Their interest was in liberation, not taxonomy.[9] Their trust in doctors was tragically abused in the interests of power and social control. Rather than liberating homosexuals, sexological discourse exchanged the prison of sin for the diagnosis of sickness (*HS*, 43–5), incarcerating same-sex desire in an intricate matrix of definitions and essentialisms which reduced homosexuals to monstrous freaks, inhabitants of a dank and dangerous hinterland between 'real' men and 'real' women. Their one redeeming feature was that, like the archetypal shy, oversensitive victim of the bully, they were good at art.

Children of the Mind

Carpenter was interested in courting societal approval for homosexuality on the strength of its cultural worth. To this end, he name-checked famous homosexuals from history and suggested that homosexuality, by its very nature, was responsible for cultural production. He argued that 'intermediates' were evolutionary superior to heterosexuals, gifted with great powers of creativity and spirituality. Because they opted out of procreation, Carpenter suggested, 'intermediates' channeled their creative energies into culture, bearing instead of bodily offspring, "children of the mind"[10]: music, poetry, art and literature. In this

---

8 See Vernon A. Rosario, 'Inversion's Histories/History's Inversions: Novelizing fin-desiecle Homosexuality' in Id., *Science and Homosexualities*, 109–18.
9 See Silverstolpe's interest-model versus power-model in 'Benkert Was Not a Doctor'.
10 Edward Carpenter, *The Intermediate Sex: A Study of Some Transitional Types of Men and Women*, George Allen & Unwin, 1908, 70. Subsequent page references will be indicated in the text by the initials *IS*.

capacity they therefore play a crucial role in the regeneration of society.

The notion of homosexuals as cultural progenitors carries with it the suggestion of cultural impoverishment in the absence of homosexuality. If the (pro)creative urge is a human universal, and its expression in heterosexuality is the birth of children, then in homosexuals, as non-breeders, one manifestation of the creative urge is the birth of art. Obviously, this is highly oversimplified, for homosexuals can of course have children, just as heterosexuals can be childless; and both can be artless (or artful). It's not a simple question of producing children or art, depending on your sexual preference. However, the idea that art can be a direct result of the sublimation of procreativity is a radical hypothesis, not only as a direct attack on the monolithic position of procreation within our culture, but also as a powerful defense of non-procreation.

More recently, it is an idea taken up by Susan Sontag in her 'Notes on Camp' (1964) and literary critic George Steiner in his essay 'Eros and Idiom' (1975). Steiner writes that: "since about 1890 homosexuality has played a vital part in Western culture and, perhaps more significantly, in the myths and emblematic gestures which that culture has used in order to arrive at self-consciousness".[11] For him, "homosexuality in part made possible that exercise in solipsism, that remorseless mockery of philistine common sense and bourgeois realism which is modern art" (*EI*, 118). This is because, according to Steiner, homosexual love constitutes a "creative rejection of the philosophic and conventional realism, of the mundanity and extroversion of classic nineteenth-century feeling"; a feeling which "produces works of art and literature which 'look outward' for their meaning and validity, which accept authorities and solicit approvals outside themselves". The homosexual reversal of this 'looking outward', an almost narcissistic 'looking inward', produces art and litera-

---

11 George Steiner, 'Eros and Idiom', in *On Difficulty and Other Essays*, Oxford University Press, 1978, 118. Subsequent page references will appear bracketed within the text, indicated by the initials *EI*. For further critique of Steiner and Sontag, see Dollimore, *Sexual Dissidence*, 307–8.

ture which is "self-sufficient", which does not court approval but rather forms a critique of the *status quo*.

Condemned forever to 'looking inward' (only possible because the homosexual is constituted as 'outside'), homosexuals, Steiner argues, create a 'sensibility' important for its critique of cultural norms, and the subsequent generation of new forms of modern culture. Carpenter, likewise, saw the children of the mind spawned by homosexuals as "the philosophical conceptions and ideals which transform our lives and those of society" (*IS*, 70, my emphasis).

In Sontag's 'Notes on Camp', she states that "the two pioneering forces of modern sensibility are Jewish moral seriousness and homosexual aestheticism and irony".[12]

Andrew Sullivan, in his book *Virtually Normal*, uses a similar argument: "One of the goods that homosexuals bring to society is undoubtedly a more highly developed sense of form, of style."[13] "Closely connected to this is a sense of irony",[14] a way of taking things less seriously, of being necessarily skeptical about everything this culture tells us. Humour plays a large – though by no means sole – part in this (lesson one: make 'em laugh before they sock you – the victim's best defense). Like Sontag, Sullivan draws a parallel with Jews, arguing that, like them, homosexuals have "developed ways to resist, subvert, and adopt a majority culture", ways of "ironizing their difference". And for Sullivan, lack of children is directly linked to this ironization, although his espousal of the cultural value of homosexuals limits itself to the more pedestrian examples of journalism, teaching and the military.[15]

---

12 Susan Sontag, 'Notes on Camp' [1964], in *The Susan Sontag Reader*, Penguin, 1982, 118. For a useful critique of Sontag's essay see D.A. Miller's 'Sontag's Urbanity' in Abelove et al. (eds), *The Lesbian and Gay Studies Reader*, 213, where he accuses her of severing camp from gay men, "all of whom are parenthetically assumed to be clones of that familiar figure of psychopathology, 'the' homosexual, with his self-evident desire to remain youthful, and the rest"; see also Moe Meyer's introduction to *The Politics and Poetics of Camp*, Routledge, 1994, in which he links the cultural form of camp to a specifically Hollywood sensibility.

13 Andrew Sullivan, *Virtually Normal: An Argument About Homosexuality*, Picador, 1996, 200.

14 Ibid.

15 Ibid., 201.

For Steiner and Sontag, then, this 'homosexual' art, style, sensibility or aesthetic – call it what you will – is contingent on the homosexual remaining outside society: a pariahdom that provokes inventive critique. Steiner and Sontag establish a direct correlation between cultural acceptance and cultural value. The exclusion of homosexuals is fruitful to heterosexual culture. Carpenter's radicalism, however, is located in his suggestion that a certain sensibility invaluable to modern culture finds its strongest conduits in homosexual men and women as non-procreative members of society, rather than as outsiders. Carpenter links cultural creation to non-procreation, whereas Steiner and Sontag see the homosexual's outsider status as the key to his/her artistic productivity or value.

Jeffrey Meyers, in his archly homophobic *Homosexuality and Literature 1890–1930*, makes a similar argument, suggesting that increased tolerance for homosexuality has led to a decrease in the quality of their fiction. Because the homosexual's chances of personal happiness are thwarted, he suggests, their spiritual or creative life must inevitably overcompensate. Paradoxically, this form of the great-homosexuals-of-history argument doesn't so much help as hinder homosexual emancipation, maintaining as it does that condescending attitude that as long as we entertain them they'll tolerate us, but only so far: we may entertain them on the doorstep, as it were, but never, ever step foot inside the house.[16]

Carpenter's strategy, however, of linking cultural production to human non-reproduction bypasses the need to perpetuate pariahdom, since the homosexual's usefulness is thus rooted elsewhere: in their lack of children, and in their confusion of gender distinctions. The former concept is straightforward enough. Freud argued much the same thing with his notion of sublimation. The latter concept, that in their blending of femi-

---

16 Simon Watney criticizes this line of argument in the context of 'gay abortion'. See his 'Gene Wars' in Maurice Berger et al. (eds), *Constructing Masculinity*, Routledge 1995, 163. For Watney, the morality of aborting on the grounds of sexuality is the issue, not whether one is aborting a Michelangelo or a Bacon. In this context, he is quite right. However, in culture that places high value on art, the contribution of homosexuals is a powerful argument in anti-homophobic discourse.

nine and masculine, intermediates exemplify a way forward for humanity by creating new types of human activity, may seem just as straightforward. But on closer inspection it proves to be more than just a little problematic.

The Good, the Bad, and the Intermediate

For Carpenter, homosexuals, or intermediates, as he called them, represent a new stage in the evolution of humanity. Like Proust, Carpenter highlights the cultural or societal role played by homosexuals; although Carpenter projects it onto a future society, a culture to come, a culture heralded by this evolutionary development of intermediates. Society should sit back and observe and learn, and allow nature to develop along its own course. As such, his argument is a plea for greater tolerance and compassion before the law. Yet, like Gide, he is clear about exactly which particular type of homosexual he is willing to defend.

Carpenter identifies two types of intermediate: a 'lower' and a 'superior' type. So far, so bad. The lower type is "extreme and exaggerated", and "often terribly sentimental"; the superior is "more normal and perfect" and "almost incredibly emotional" (*IS*, 13; 29). (Elsewhere, "extreme" is used in opposition to "healthy" in Carpenter's nomination of the two types of intermediate, and therefore equated with unhealthiness [*IS*, 37]).[17] Carpenter delineates extreme cases of the inferior type (inverts), whom, while being "of the greatest value from a scientific point of view as marking tendencies and limits of development in certain directions", must on no account be looked upon as "representative cases of the whole phase of human evolution concerned" (*IS*, 32). Carpenter leaves no doubt as to who these lower types are: those men and women who display cross-gender behaviour. He regards these specimens as "not particularly

---

17 Carpenter's argument is compromised somewhat by the contradiction between his statement that "individuals affected with inversion in marked degree do not after all differ from the rest of mankind, or womankind, in any other physical or mental particular which can be distinctly indicated"; and his claim in the footnote attached to this sentence, that "there is no doubt a general *tendency* towards femininity of type in the male Urning, and towards masculinity in the female" (*IS*, 57, original emphasis). We might ask, when does a tendency become a characteristic?

attractive, sometimes quite the reverse" (*IS*, 30). In the case of men, effeminacy is the *bête noire,* and Carpenter describes a by now familiar figure:

> Sentimental, lackadaisical, mincing in gait and manners, something of a chatterbox, skilful at the needle and in woman's work, sometimes taking pleasure in dressing in woman's clothes; his figure not unfrequently betraying a tendency towards the feminine, large at the hips, supple, not muscular, the face wanting in hair, the voice inclining to be high-pitched, etc; while his dwelling-room is orderly in the extreme, even natty, and choice of decoration and perfume. His affection, too, is often feminine in character, clinging, dependent and jealous, as of one desiring to be loved almost more than to love (*IS*, 30)

There is a profound anxiety at work here over what constitutes being a man and what constitutes being a woman, with a clear understanding that the effeminate homosexual is not a man (he's not a woman, either, but some grotesque hybrid or mockery of the two, clearly, in Carpenter's mind). And yet effeminacy can just as easily be a heterosexual trait. (Indeed, until the last decade of the nineteenth century, it by no means exclusively connoted same-sex desire[18]). If effeminacy is now almost exclusively associated with homosexual men, this is more likely the result of the establishment of a medical model which posits the gay man as the possessor of a female soul, and the translation of that medical model into a cultural model. Effeminacy has become the most overworked and culturally identifiable sign for representing homosexuality: a stereotype, bearing, at best, a fantasy relation to reality. In reality, effeminacy has no grounding in the gestures of women, and such gestures are not the expression of an essential femininity, anyway, but the consequence of acculturation. Furthermore, homosexuals are as exposed to acculturation as heterosexuals, and internalize the monolithic notions of

---

[18] See Sinfield, *The Wilde Century.*

masculinity and femininity peddled by the media just as much as heterosexuals, if not more so (after all, one becomes more aware of the law when one is breaking it). Effeminacy, therefore, emerges as a set of highly problematic gestures culturally available to any body, regardless of biological sex or sexual preference, even if the target for its use as a tool for oppression is invariably gay men (see chapter two).

By allowing his superior intermediates to be defined in opposition to these 'extreme cases', even though he claims that the latter constitute a minority, Carpenter is abetting the maintenance of a discursively visible and resilient stereotype. Rather than being seen as revealing the limits of the naturalizing discourse on gender, these extreme cases of femme queens and butch dykes are seen by Carpenter as revealing the limits of cross-gender behaviour. They represent for him nature gone awry rather than the entire artificiality of gender roles. Like Gide, Carpenter insists on the scarcity of effeminate homosexuals, yet cannot resist invoking them in homophobic and self-oppressed terms, establishing an ethics of homosexuality which standardizes normative gender behaviour. A code of conduct is clearly established which polices behaviour and constrains pleasure. Indulgence in sexual please is a sign of inferiority, effeminacy, and degeneracy, a liminality apparent in the salient physiognomy: "large at the hips", "supple, not muscular, faces wanting in hair, the voice inclining to be high-pitched"; a creature straight out of the nineteenth century freak show; the product of a culture so obsessed with sustaining an unrealistic dimorphic gender system that it panics, bristles with paranoia and disgust, in the presence of bodies that defy such facile categorization.

The question is: "Can a male be homosexual, combine with another male, without a loss of virility?"[19] The ever-present spectre of feminisation haunts relations between men. The intermediate male must infuse his masculinity with the right amount of femininity (emotional but not sentimental), for there will always be the ideological danger that "the feminine will supplant

---
19 John Fletcher, 'Forster's self-erasure: Maurice and the scene of masculine love', in Joseph Bristow (ed.), *Sexual Sameness*, Routledge, 1992, 74.

or improperly dominate the masculine in the mixed type, that instead of an extension of the masculine beyond its traditional sphere a subversion of the masculine may result",[20] and Carpenter's extreme cases bear witness to this danger.

Carpenter's superior type of intermediate, unsurprisingly, is masculine in appearance: "fine, healthy specimens of their sex, muscular and well-developed in body, of powerful brain, high standard of conduct, and with nothing abnormal or morbid of any kind observable in their physical structure or constitution" (*IS*, 23). Given such idealization, surely this type is in the minority: how many human beings – gay or straight – meet such exacting criteria of perfection? Carpenter insists on their strength, their muscularity, their similarity in appearance to their straight counterparts (yet how many straight men are strong, muscular with powerful brains?[21]). But, unlike the heterosexual male – whom Carpenter describes as an "ungrown, half-baked sort of character"[22] – these beings are "extremely complex" emotionally, "tender, sensitive, pitiful and loving" (*IS*, 33).

This superior intermediate male, then, is a being clearly unlike the third sex, although it does represent some hybrid form between complete masculinity and complete femininity. Moreover, it is only this superior type which will, Carpenter is certain, have "an important part to play in the transformation" of society to a higher form (*IS*, 122–3). Like Gide, Carpenter's interest and concern for the inferior type is scant. He consolidates Western medicine's most reductionist assumptions about gender, maintaining that extreme cross-gendering is most threateningly embodied in effeminate homosexuals and masculine lesbians.

While he vehemently denies a direct link between 'homogenic' love and degeneracy, Carpenter's condemnation is riddled with anxiety, fear and moral superiority. It is also grounded in normative assumptions of fixed gender categories. The Victorian era, during which Carpenter had grown to adulthood, was

---
20 Ibid.
21 Miller, in *Bringing Out Roland Barthes*, writes very well on this aspect of gay male embodiment, "as *the body that can fuck, fuck you over*" (30–1, original emphasis).
22 Carpenter, 'Man, the Ungrown', in *Selected Writings*, 1.110.

characterized by a hyperbolic paranoia and panic over the dissolution of traditional gender roles, responses Showalter sees as typical of the fin de siècle: "in periods of cultural insecurity, when there are fears of regression and degeneration, the longing for strict border controls around the definition of gender [...] becomes especially intense".[23]

The messianic, regenerating potential of the superior intermediate is seriously threatened by the degenerating inferior type. The former are assumed to be "the teachers of future society" (IS, 14), each one "a rare and beautiful flower of humanity" (IS, 11), whereas the latter can teach us nothing, every last one of them "a perverse and tangled ruin" (IS, 11). Both being figments of Carpenter's imagination, neither was particularly useful in the real world, obscuring the conditions of real life. More: these two extremes constitute a polarity which fails to represent the plurality of sexual expression. Whilst being ridiculously utopic, Carpenter's theory was by no means homotopic.[24]

Just a Phase

Carpenter suggests a curious logic to nature's gender blending: the intermediate's role is to ensure that the two sexes – the two ends of the gender spectrum – do not "drift into far latitudes and absolutely cease to understand each other" (IS, 17). In other words, homosexuality ensures the harmoniousness of heterosexuality. Like Tiresias, the intermediate has access to two gender worlds, containing "such a union or balance of the feminine and masculine qualities" that he or she is able to negotiate between men and women and repair differences, act as an "[interpreter] of men and women to each other" (IS, 18). Without homosexuals to smooth over the cracks, heterosexuality, Carpenter suggests,

---

23 Showalter, *Sexual Anarchy*, 4, esp. ch. 9: 'Decadence, Homosexuality and Feminism'.
24 Of course, it's easy for us to sit in our privileged position of historical hindsight and ridicule Carpenter's naivety, but more importantly, his evolutionary argument offered proto-homosexuals a secure haven for their fragile identities, only to pull the rug from under them. According to Carpenter's theory, they were a dying breed, pawns of nature useful only temporarily. What kind of politicized identity could such an instability produce? Alternatively, Carpenter was right but the human race remains far from perfect, so until it is, queers are here to stay.

would soon break down, "for indeed no one else can possibly respond to and understand, as they do, all the fluctuations and interactions of the masculine and feminine in human life" (*IS*, 121). One is left to imagine some poor queen flitting between an estranged husband and wife trying his best to appease them both, much like Proust's Charlus acting as a go-between for the quarrelling lovers, Swann and Odette. The deep condescension inherent in such an image hardly needs pointing out.

As well as this male–female continuum, Carpenter also maps a Kinsey-esque sliding scale of "all possible grades of sexual inversion":

> From that in which the instinct is quite exclusively directed towards the same sex, to the other extreme in which it is normally towards the opposite sex but capable, occasionally and under exceptional attractions, of inversion towards its own – this last condition being probably among some peoples very widespread, if not universal. (*IS*, 56)

The terrain being mapped out here is becoming increasingly fraught with problems. Several inconsistencies or questions arise:
1. What are we evolving towards? Greater tolerance for sexual dissidence? Or everyone becoming intermediate?
2. Does Carpenter believe all human beings are essentially bisexual? If so, where does this leave intermediates, not to mention their pariahdom and its rich seam of cultural critique?
3. What are the mechanisms of this evolution? If intermediates are almost exclusively homosexual, it cannot be by sexual transmission. If there is such open hostility towards intermediates, can such an evolutionary change be seen as natural? Does the rest of humanity need convincing before such change can be implemented (which rather negates the idea of it being evoluntionary)?
4. The task would seem to have devolved onto nature, yet what does nature have to gain by making everyone intermediate? Carpenter, in this sense, is positing an anti-evolutionary,

somewhat genocidal (we might say *homo*cidal) politics (fear of a queer planet, indeed!).
5. Carpenter's theory suggests merely an historical transcience for homosexuality. If intermediate types are an "indication of some important change actually in progress" (*IS*, 11), by which "certain new types of human kind may be emerging", then what to make of the results of such an evolutionary change? Once the utopia promised by the existence of these messianic beings has been achieved, what function would intermediates serve? Would they expire like the dinosaurs? Or would all humans become (superior) intermediate types? All Carpenter has to say on the matter is, "We do not know" (*IS*, 11).

Even Carpenter's neologism for homosexuals – intermediate – suggests a temporary stage rather than a termination, a point on a journey to somewhere rather than a destination, or 'a substance formed during one of the stages of a chemical process before the desired product is obtained' (OED). Carpenter's employment of the word intermediate certainly implies both this sense of human transformation or evolution, and the idea that the intermediate was a halfway point between exclusive maleness and exclusive femaleness. Moreover, by introducing a hierarchical two-tier system by which Uranians could be judged, and promoting the notion of superior intermediates as a kind of Master Race (remember his "rare and beautiful flowers of humanity" versus the "perverse and tangled ruin"), Carpenter was skating dangerously close to eugenics.[25] His explicit loathing for the inferior type carries with it an implicit desire for their eradication. His stereotypes of chattering queens doing needlepoint and butch lesbians hunting and smoking pipes are paraded as examples of how not to be a homosexual; a rigid code of sexual conduct emerges against which homosexuals are judged and categorized as good or bad – even, or maybe especially by each other. But the how and why of sexual conduct contain what Sue

---

25 Sheila Rowbotham also accuses Carpenter of articulating eugenicist ideas (see n. 33, below). For a brief history of the British eugenics movement see Germaine Greer, *Sex & Destiny: The Politics of Human Fertility*, Picador, 1984, 155–294.

Golding has called the Trojan Horse Dilemma, whereby the assumption of what is to be proven is embedded in the given.

> These twin problems of 'the how to' and 'the why' of sexual comportment and its resulting moral codes, usually do no better than to take as a given what it is they are trying to prove, and then make us live up to it, to boot, or get mad at us if we don't, or think there is some profound Reason if we do some of it most of the time and none of it the rest.[26]

The effort to be oneself becomes mediated by regulations governing the self one is to be: identity is policed.

For Carpenter, the assumptions he brought to his grounding of 'truth' were a biological fixity to sexual behaviour. "The assumption that sexual behaviour was grounded in biology prevented Carpenter from seeing sexual stereotypes as malleable and socially constructed."[27] Clearly unable to think outside of the gender binarisms of his day – "to free sexuality from the tyranny of gender"[28] – he accepted the traditional allocation of certain traits as feminine and others as masculine, without ever questioning that these might be socially implemented behaviours rather than biologically determined characteristics. Although he rejected the notion that homosexual men must by their very nature be feminine in appearance, he foreclosed a real critique of the social aspect of gender by assuming that femininity and masculinity were fixed, with the result that the "androgynous intermediate sex became just another fixed stereotype, albeit some mixture of the two extremes".[29]

The category of 'sexual intermediate' emerges as a dubiously infirm foundation for any secure ontological structure: a shifting ground, always already metamorphosising into some new type of human, some unknown mixture between male and female,

---
26 Sue Golding, 'Sexual Manners', in *Public* 8 (1993), 164.
27 Sheila Rowbotham, 'Edward Carpenter: Prophet of the New Life', in Rowbotham and Weeks (eds), *Socialism and the New Life*, 111.
28 Ibid.
29 Beverley Thiele 'Coming-of-Age: Edward Carpenter on Sex & Reproduction', in T. Brown (ed.), *Edward Carpenter and Late Victorian Radicalism*, Cass, 1990, 109.

some formless identity; a chaotic borderland where nothing is safe, nothing is known and paranoia breeds. That explanation familiar to any queer teenager, that it's *just a phase*,[30] springs to mind here, employed as an evolutionist apology for a behaviour deemed culturally unacceptable.

The Best of Both Worlds?

Although the political implications of Carpenter's intermediate ideal are often read as potentially pro-homosexual, his insistence on the fixed attributes of gender have been seen as anti-feminist.[31] He perpetuated traditional ideas about femininity, taking for granted those traits traditionally attached to women. He saw woman as a higher form, believing their emotional superiority to be the way forward, so for him women who manifested manly gestures signified a devolution, a degeneration. As such, his theory holds no value for lesbians. His intermediate ideal possessed the exterior of a man and the interior of a woman; a muscular physique coupled with a sensitive nature.[32] He wrote nothing about the female counterpart.[33]

Carpenter referred to this ideal form of humanity as "the double life", best described as a form of androgyny, although the cross-genderisation is not a physical manifestation – remember his superior Uranian has a muscular physique. Rather, it is an idealized balance of the masculine and the feminine and is rep-

---

30 In the early 90s a lesbian and gay lifestyle magazine chose the name *Phaze* in an ironic reappropriation of such an accusation, only to be condemned to such transcience itself, folding after half a dozen issues.

31 See both Thiele, 'Coming-of-Age' and Rowbotham, 'Edward Carpenter' on this score.

32 This is a variation on Ulrichs' formula, although Carpenter dismissed Ulrichs' idea because of his use of words such as 'soul' and 'body' – words which Carpenter saw as "somewhat vague and indefinite" (*IS*, 20). The words 'pot', 'kettle' and 'black' spring to mind.

33 According to Rowbotham, lesbians were omitted from Carpenter's future race: "the democratic vision of affective sexuality extending itself through the world becomes narrowed to an elite, a superior brotherhood." In Rowbotham's view, Carpenter appears as some kind of proto-fascist, condoning certain forms of gender behaviour, condemning others; a view that isn't altogether inaccurate. "Even within his own terms Carpenter's notion of transcendent androgyny remained remarkably sex-bound. It was all very well for men to carry fixed feminine characteristics and gain a power to see through the divide between the sexes. But it appears to go wrong when it is applied to women in practice" (Rowbotham, 'Edward Carpenter', 112).

resentative of a new form of life: the best of both worlds. But as Rowbotham warns: "an androgynous stereotype ignores how all our notions of what a man is and what a woman is are created by the totality of our social relationships and by the circumstances of our own sexual practice".[34] Androgyny goes beyond sexual difference and threatens to disavow the demarcations of cross-sex versus same-sex desire. For homosexuality, like heterosexuality, requires sexual difference for its very existence. If being homosexual is predicated on a desire for one's own sex, then it is a preference/orientation[35] contingent on two categories of human being: men and women. Androgyny, in confusing or blending sexual difference, makes categories such as homosexual and heterosexual redundant (or at the very least problematic). If we were all androgynous to the extent that 'men' and 'women' no longer existed as social categories in which to slot biologically sexed bodies, how would you know whether the person you were attracted to had a penis or a vagina? And more to the point, would it matter? (Carpenter himself was revolted by effeminacy, preferring muscular, working-class men[36]).

So, in striving for the 'double life' of androgyny, was Carpenter striving for an end to the great homo/hetero divide? Was he calling for a deconstruction of gender boundaries and the building of a new life in which gender would no longer be the diacritical marker of sexual difference or preference, an egalitarian land where so-called feminine gestures and attributes can become the gestures and attributes of men, and vice versa?

In a word: no.

---

34 Ibid., 111.
35 There is much debate about whether homosexuality is an orientation or a preference, the former term suggesting innateness, the latter choice. To avoid going into the debate, I have included both terms. Delete as appropriate. For a fuller account of the debate see Vera Whisman, *Queer By Choice: Lesbians, Gay Men and the Politics of Identity*, Routledge, 1996, pp 40–41; Edward Stein, 'Conclusion: The Essentials of Constructionism and the Construction of Essentialism', in Id. (ed.), *Forms of Desire: Sexual Orientation and the Social Constructionist Controversy*, Routledge, 1992.
36 Carpenter, 'Self-Analysis for Havelock Ellis', in *Selected Writings*, 1.290. Bersani writes very provocatively on what he calls "the erotic complicity of gay men in the very representations of masculinity that exclude us". See his 'Loving Men', in Berger et al. (eds), *Constructing Masculinity*, 113–23.

The superior type of intermediate, in whose combination of big muscles and sensitivity Carpenter saw – through heavily rose-tinted glasses, it has to be said – a "union or balance of the feminine and masculine qualities" (IS, 18), carries with it a belief in fixed gender types which does nothing to deconstruct the notion of homosexuals as harbingers of gender dysphoria and sovereign symbols of "a range of deep failures including the demise of masculinity, the abdication of masculine power, the desire for self-destruction, and, beyond that, the loss of difference".[37] In short, the only possible desire governing one's choice to be sodomized must be a desire for self-annihilation,[38] and the self that one is annihilating is masculine. The price one pays for enjoying a penis in one's rectum is one's masculinity (which is, within patriarchy, beyond value).

Taking the Sex Out

Carpenter considered homosexual to be a heteroclite term, "a bastard word" (IS, 40n), because it mixed Greek (*homos*) with Latin (*sexualis*), preferring instead his own invention, homogenic, deriving from two Greek words, *homos* (same) and *genos* (sex). More significantly, the term homogenic suggests genetics rather than sexuality, taking the 'sex' out of same-sex relationships. Which is exactly what Carpenter did. In *The Intermediate Sex* he argues that in general it is inaccurate to suppose that homogenic attachments "are necessarily sexual, or connected with sexual acts" (IS, 26). He draws a distinction between sexual libertines, who indulge in homosexuality out of "a mere carnal curiosity" (IS, 50), and Uranians, who are "often purely emotional in their character" (IS, 26), and who are driven by "a genuine heart-attachment" (IS, 50). Like Gide, Carpenter also denies that anal intercourse is at all common amongst Uranians. Appealing to Krafft-Ebing's writing on the subject, he claims that "the special act with which they are vulgarly credited is in most cases repug-

---
37 Dollimore, *Sexual Dissidence*, 263.
38 See Bersani, 'Is the Rectum a Grave?' for a discussion of the 'suicidal ecstacy' and shattering of the self involved, according to Bersani, in a man's adoption of the receptive role in anal sex.

nant to them" (IS, 58). In response to the *British Medical Journal*'s caustic review of *The Intermediate Sex*, Carpenter wrote:

> I am certain there is not a single passage in the book where I advocate sexual intercourse of any kind between those of the same sex. I advocate sincere attachment and warm friendship, and allow that this may have fitting expression in 'caress and embrace' – but I suppose that to some minds this is sufficient, and it is immediately interpreted as an advocacy of lust.[39]

Unlike Gide, whose separation of sex from procreation foregrounds a natural, animalistic desire for physical pleasure, Carpenter's foregrounds spirituality at the expense of any form of *jouissance*; a stance much like the one taken today by the Church of England: it's okay to be gay as long as you're celibate. A stylistics of existence around homosexuality begins to emerge which is incapable of dealing with the plain fact of sexual pleasure. Desire is acceptable, so long as it is controlled. Pleasure is unforgivable. According to Foucault, desire has been "used as a tool, as a grid of intelligibility, a calibration in terms of normality", whereas pleasure "passes from one individual to another […]. [It] has no passport, no identification papers."[40]

In his case study for Havelock Ellis' *Sexual Inversion*, Carpenter confesses to never having indulged in "actual pederasty, so called". He claims to being able to conceive of anal sex – "either active or passive" – only with "one [he] loved very devotedly and who also loved [him] to that degree".[41] He details his "chief desire in love" as "bodily nearness or contact". For Carpenter "the specially sexual, though urgent enough, seems a secondary matter".[42] The primary matter was the spiritual, for this allowed

---

39 Quoted in Weeks, *Coming Out*, 81.
40 Quoted in Halperin, *Saint Foucault*, 95.
41 Carpenter, 'Self-Analysis', 290.
42 Ibid. See Spencer, *Homosexuality*, 301-2, for an account of how Carpenter seduced a man sixty years his junior. Gavin Arthur was taken to see Carpenter in the 1920s, and asked him if he had slept with Walt Whitman. Carpenter said yes. Arthur asked how Whitman had made love. Carpenter said, "I'll show you." Spencer writes: "They went to bed together, naked beneath the eiderdown, first holding hands and lying on their backs, then Carpenter kissed his ear and began to fondle his body very lightly, ignoring

him to argue the case from a more evolutionary and less 'prurient' position. Whether he genuinely placed little importance on the sexual aspect of comrade love, or whether he saw it as a political move to shift the debate away from an exclusive focus on the specificity of certain sexual acts, Carpenter's emphasis on the spiritual gave his politics an idealism (not to mention prudery) rendered virtually impracticable by the real lives of gay men and lesbians as people who have sex.

I would suggest that the term 'homosocial' is a far more accurate description of the type of same-sex relationship advocated by Carpenter. And as Sedgwick has show, homosociality is violently opposed to homosexuality, the two categories rigidly and phobically kept apart, the former systematically policed for traces of the latter, because "for a man to be a man's man is separated only by an invisible, carefully blurred, always-already-crossed line from being 'interested in men'".[43] Carpenter projects

---

the lad's genitalia, but licking, 'flickering all over me like summer lightning'. This went on for some time and Arthur became excited, having an orgasm just at the moment that Carpenter fellated him. 'The emphasis was on the caressing and loving. I fell asleep like a child safe in father-mother arms, the arms of God.'" Whether Carpenter shared Whitman's style and never went further than this kind of massage, we do not know. But sodomy was clearly off the menu.

43 Sedgwick, *Between Men*, 89. She continues: "Those terms, those congruences, are by now endemic and perhaps ineradicable in our culture" (89–90). The concept of homosociality has been extremely useful in formulating my ideas on Carpenter and the period in which he was writing, a time when relationships between men were fraught with dangers. Sedgwick argues that our homosocial culture projects onto the abject body of the homosexual the desires which cannot be articulated within patriarchal-heterosexual relationships between men, relationships based on domination and a repudiation of erotic bonds. Jane Gallop (via Irigaray) claims something similar: "Irigaray has discovered that phallic, sexual theory, male sexual science, is homosexual, a sexuality of sames, of identities, excluding otherness. Heterosexuality, once it is exposed as an exchange of women between men, reveals itself as a mediated form of homosexuality. All penetration [...] is thought according to the model of anal penetration. The dry anus suffers pain: the penetrated is a humiliated man" (*Feminism and Psychoanalysis: The Daughter's Seduction*, Macmillan, 1982, 84–5). Aside from the straightforward homophobia in this passage, one is tempted to write to its author advising some form of lubrication. If patriarchy were simply a sublimated form of homosexuality, then why aren't homosexuals acceptable within patriarchy? Surely by doing without women, gay men are the apotheosis of patriarchal thought? Whereas Sedgwick usefully distinguishes between homosociality (which is a prerequisite of patriarchy) and homosexuality (which is not), Irigaray and Gallop confuse the two, which is no aid at all in attempting to untie the knot of problems surrounding the denigration of the female (not only women, but also the female in men, most typically read as homosexual – especially anal receptiveness), the sublimation of desire between heterosexual men versus the accen-

any erotic bonds onto a proscribed inferior type of intermediate, whilst condemning the superior type to a life of caress and embrace. Sexuality here is seen as highly destructive to sociality. The social is undermined by the sexual, and the projection onto homosexuals of an exaggerated sexuality which threatens sociality begins to make sense in a culture with such a high investment in the containment of sexuality.

Sedgwick's definition of homophobia as "a mechanism for regulating the behaviour of the many by the specific oppression of a few"[44] reveals Carpenter's own ethics as deeply homophobic. For, doesn't he advocate a regulation of all homosexuals by oppressing the activity of a few, i.e., those who indulge in anal sex? He separates sexuality from procreation only to dilute it into oblivion. By denying that sex played a significant role in the lives of homosexuals (and if sex did occur, it was most definitely not anal), Carpenter maintained a shamefulness about gay sex which has proved hard to shake off.

By privileging the existence of the virile, healthy and distinctly asexual homosexual, Carpent is guilty of a certain complicity, of merely reiterating and reinforcing the assumption that anal sex was a practice only indulged in by the degenerate and effeminate, and that true homosexuality had nothing to do with it – true homosexuals being musclebound eneuchs who satisfy themselves with mere 'caress and embrace'. In Carpenter's thesis, desire for the same becomes nothing more than a form of narcissism because the traditional theories of desire turn on the notion of difference. Yet to desire the same sex is not to desire the self. And this is not because, within sexological discourse, the desiring self for a homosexual is feminine, but because homosexuality should be understood as a desire *between men*.

Why was this so impossible? What Symonds, in the next chapter, calls *l'amour de l'impossible*?

---

tuation of desire between gay men (we're all assumed to do it with anyone at any given opportunity), and the distribution of power within patriarchal society.

44 Sedgwick, *Between Men*, 88.

Chapter Four

A Problem in Gay Heroics
John Addington Symonds and l'amour de l'impossible

> "When the whole interest of a life centres, not in action, but in mental development and moral experience, truth becomes imperatively necessary with regard to points of apparent insignificance."
> – Symonds, *Memoirs*

Why did the Victorian poet and essayist John Addington Symonds (1840–1893) call love between men the love of the impossible? What did he consider so impossible about it, and how did the discourse that emerged around homosexuality at the end of the nineteenth century foreclose the possibility of love between men?

We have seen how in Gide and Carpenter, the sexual element of same-sex love was secondary to a stylistics of existence. In this way, homosexuality as an identity became much more significant than as a sexual proclivity or desire, the sexual act less important than the personality type which became increasingly associated with it. We have also seen how, in Proust especially, the concept of same-sex attraction was subordinated within a heterosexual matrix in which a man's desire for other men always derives from an immanent femininity. In a similar manner to Carpenter, Symonds attempted to masculinise homosexual love, and this chapter explores the ways in which he tried to do this, but failed, because of the impossibility of accommodating same-sex desire within heterological concepts of desire. For this reason, the homosexual discourse was characterized by anxieties around issues of private/public, knowledge/ignorance, subjectivity/objectivity, from its very inception, with Symonds, one of the first people to theorise about same-sex love.

Like Carpenter, Symonds is seen as a pioneer of a health model of homosexuality, and yet his *Memoirs* express the feeling that he was suffering from an incurable sickness. Between these two statements, where can we locate the truth of homosexuality and its emergence into discourse? How did the initial discursive appearance of a homosexual *type* relate not only to a medical discourse but also to actual lived experience? How can we make sense of this apparent contradiction?

The Effect of an Eccentric

The *Memoirs* of John Addington Symonds, written in the 1890s but not published until 1984, bear the curious subtitle, *The Secret Homosexual Life of a Leading Nineteenth Century Man of Letters*. The secret homosexual life? Anyone familiar with the figure of Symonds and his role in homosexual history (see, for example, Weeks' *Coming Out*) will find it odd that Symonds' homosexuality could be referred to as secret. True, it would have been foolish to parade publically one's sexuality in the light of the Labouchere Amendment of 1885, which criminalized 'acts of gross indecency' between men with a sentence of up to two years' hard labour, but Symonds has earned a place in gay history as a pioneer, not a man with a secret homosexual life. His writing alluded to it, his close friends were aware of it, and as far as it was possible at the time to live as a gay man, Symonds did; so where's the secret? Bristow refers to the open secret of Symonds' homosexuality within his circle of friends.[1] According to D.A. Miller, secrecy can function as

> The subjective practice in which the oppositions of private/public, inside/outside, subject/object are established, and the sanctity of their first term kept inviolate. And the phenomenon of the 'open secret' does not, as one might think, bring

---

[1] Joseph Bristow, *Effeminate England: Homoerotic Writing After 1885*, Open University Press, 1995, 128.

about the collapse of those binarisms and their ideological effects, but rather attests to their fantasmatic recovery.[2]

For Symonds, as for lesbians and gay men today, the disclosure of one's sexuality is a constantly negotiable event. By shifting the responsibility of the fate of his memoirs onto his literary executor, Symonds avoided such a negotiation. The real secret, for students of gay history, is the revelation of Symonds' true feelings about his homosexual desire, which he describes in the memoirs as a "congenital aberration of the passions", which had been "the poison of [his] life".[3] In public, he was perceived as a political figure, aligned with the aesthetic movement, socialist thought and progressive ideas. In private, he regarded his homosexuality to be an innate sickness from which his abilities as a writer and thinker suffered immeasurably. The ideological effects of the private/public divide are thus fantasmatically recovered, and the crisis of definition is anxiously aroused.[4]

Symonds was acutely aware of the assumed objectivity of science and the so-called subjectivity of literature. When he was scouting for someone with whom he could write a book on inversion, he admitted to Carpenter, "I need somebody of medical importance to collaborate with. Alone, I could make but little effect – the effect of an eccentric."[5] The man he approached for this collaboration was Havelock Ellis, a young heterosexual doctor just then making a name for himself in the field of sexology. The pair never met, but the collaborative result of their correspondence was *Sexual Inversion,* published in 1897, one of the first works on homosexuality to appear in English (although it was originally published in German due to an obscenity charge). Symonds avoided accusations of indecency by speci-

---

2 D.A. Miller, *The Novel and the Police,* University of California Press, 1988, 207.
3 John A. Symonds, T*he Memoirs of John Addington Symonds: The Secret Homosexual Life of a Leading Nineteenth-Century Man of Letters,* ed.Phyllis Grosskurth, Random House, 1984, 190. Subsequent page references appear in brackets, indicated by the abbreviation M.
4 Sedgwick, *Epistemology of the Closet,* 72.
5 Symonds in a letter to Carpenter, 29 December 1892, in Herbert M. Schueller & Robert L. Peters (eds), *The Letters of John Addington Symonds,* vol. 3, Wayne State University Press, 1969, 797.

fying his readership: men interested in scientific phenomenon. In his *Memoirs,* the chapter dealing with his homosexuality is entitled 'Containing material which none but students of psychology and ethics need peruse' (M, 61); everyone else should move on to the next chapter to avoid offence or confusion – this is esoteric stuff.

Symonds is adopting the highbrow tones of the doctor, and for understandable reasons. Sexology "promised to be a forgiving branch of an implacably homophobic culture"; like Gide, "he longed to blend his voice with the impeccable tones of the doctor"[6] to avoid accusations of prurience or, worse, partisanship. The guise of a doctor replaces subjectivity with objectivity, and the homosexual's own voice becomes subordinate to the authoritative voice of medicine. The reverse discourse was not allowed to function independently; it was contingent on theories and vocabulary and protocols set down by the medical discourse. Like a colonized race learning the master language before being able to articulate dissent, Symonds et al. only had at their disposal the language of science with which to work towards legitimacy.

Symonds' death in 1893 not only meant he missed the Wilde trials and their horrific impact on the lives of English homosexuals, it also meant he did not see the project with Ellis through to completion and publication. After his death, his writings on homosexuality were suppressed by his literary executor, Horatio Brown, and his role in the writing of *Sexual Inversion* was effectively erased. However, the nature of discourse clearly works in the face of such erasure, as evidenced by the anonymity of the case histories which constituted the foundation of medical observation. These authorless narratives supply the experiential data upon which medical knowledge was based.

Symonds both resists the medical insistence on sickness whilst *at the same time* articulating it to explain and defend his sense of same-sex desire as somehow at the very core of his being: "a fierce rejection of the physician's pathological etiol-

---

6   Wayne Koestenbaum, *Double Talk: The Erotics of Male Literary Collaboration*, Routledge, 1989, 43–44.

ogy" *and* an "acceptance of it as a scientific alibi for his profile of himself having a distinct, inescapable identity".[7] In his correspondence with Ellis Symonds expresses great concern that collaborating with a doctor will present homosexuality in the wrong light, whilst also offering the only valid mode of objective representation.[8]

In a letter to Horatio Brown Symonds refers to the *Memoirs* as having a unique value in its "disclosure of a type of man who has *not yet been classified*" (M, 289); a curious comment when one considers that by the time Symonds wrote the autobiography he was well aware of the medical profession's zealous taxonomy of inverts/Urnings/homosexuals. Indeed, he could be said to have contributed to such classification with his collaboration with Ellis. Was he, perhaps, referring to the *self*-classification rather than the taxonomic tagging from above, explicitly foregrounding the reversal of discourse which Foucault was later to theorize? Perhaps this hitherto unclassified type was the non-effeminate homosexual, which type Symonds seems to have been, and which medical science ignored in favour of those examples which supported the third sex/inversion theory because it was more in line with their theories of perversion and degeneration.

In the *Memoirs* he describes himself both within and against Ulrichs' taxonomics:

> With regard to Ulrichs, in his peculiar phraseology, I should certainly be tabulated as a *Mittel Urning,* holding a mean between the *Mannling* and the *Weibling*; that is to say, one whose emotions are directed to the male sex during the period of adolescence and early manhood; who is not marked either by an effeminate passion for robust adults or by a predilection for young boys; in other words, one whose comradely instincts are tinged with a distinct sexual partiality. But in this sufficiently accurate description of my attitude, I do not recognize anything which justifies the theory of a

---

7   Rudi C. Bleys, *The Geography of Perversion: Male-to-male Sexual Behaviour outside the West and the Ethnographic Imagination 1750–1918*, Cassell, 1997, 209.
8   See Koestenbaum, *Double Talk*, 43–67.

female soul. Morally and intellectually, in character and taste and habits, I am more masculine than many men I know who adore women. I have no feminine feeling for the males who rouse my desire (M, 65)

In Urlichs' taxonomy, a Mannling is a masculine homosexual, a Weibling an effeminate one. Symonds explicitly challenges the medical association of 'feminine feeling' with a desire for males, and yet his desire for "sound and vigorous young men of a lower rank"[9] suggests an idealization of working class masculinity which contrasts with his own class position and personal ill-health. Like Carpenter and Forster, he never chose male lovers from his own class. Describing a pick-up with a grenadier, Symonds contrasts himself – "a slight nervous man of fashion in [his] dress clothes" – with the "strapping fellow in a scarlet uniform", Symonds "strongly attracted by his physical magnetism" (M, 186). A lifetime of illness would seem to have led Symonds to associate his own homosexual desire with sickness, and the objects of his desire with health. While health=masculinity, sickness=femininity. Although Symonds contests the notion of 'feminine feeling', he associated his sickness (both his physical maladies and his homosexuality) with a lack of masculinity and virility.

Regarding the *Memoirs,* Symonds was torn between being "anxious [...] that this document should not perish", and desiring that it not be "injurious to my family".[10] He wrote: "I have to think of the world's verdict – since I have given pledges to the future in the shape of my four growing girls."[11] (One of his daughters, Katherine, demanded access to the manuscript in 1949, but there is no record of her response to the revelations therein[12]). Unsure how to solve the problem, he left it to his executor, Brown, to decide. Brown published a biography

---

9   Printed as Appendix One in M, 287.
10 Quoted from a letter to H. F. Brown 29 December 1891, printed as Appendix Two in M, 289.
11 Phyllis Grosskurth, *John Addington Symonds: A Biography,* Longmans, Green & Co Ltd, 1964, 277.
12 Ibid., 275.

of Symonds two years after his death composed almost entirely of extracts from the *Memoirs,* but with all references to his homosexuality excised, thus negating the book's very *raison d'être.* On Brown's death, in 1926, the manuscript went to the London Library with a fifty-year ban on publication.

Symonds complained towards the end of his life that he had never properly spoken out on homosexuality.[13] Considering that Symonds never truly intended the autobiography to be published, one would expect a more explicit account of his homosexuality than one actually finds. Even the anonymous case study of himself included in *Sexual Inversion* is reticent about what he actually did with other men, but is more concerned with the genealogy of his homosexual desire. But like the above passage from the *Memoirs,* he refutes any effeminacy: "He is certainly not simply passive and shows no signs of *effeminatio*. He likes sound and vigorous young men of a lower rank from the age of 20 to 25. I gather from his conversation that the mode of pleasure is indifferent to his tastes."[14] Like Carpenter, Symonds denies any indulgence in sodomy ('certainly not simply passive"). The message is clear in both cases: sodomy is for cissies. The association of being "simply passive" with *effeminatio* bears witness to the constant anxiety around anal sex as feminizing, as well as effeminacy being seen as the sure sign of passivity.

Koestenbaum points out the subtle yet poignant differences between one scene in the case history and its corresponding description in the *Memoirs*; namely, Symonds' erotic daydreams of naked sailors:

> Among my earliest recollections I must record certain visions, half-dream, half-reverie, which were certainly erotic in their nature, and which recurred frequently just before sleeping. I used to fancy myself crouched upon the floor amid a company of naked adult men: sailors, such as I had seen about the streets of Bristol. The contact of their bodies afforded me a vivid and mysterious pleasure. (M, 62)

---

13 Grosskurth, in her Forward to M, 11.
14 Printed as Appendix One in M, 287–8.

> About the age of 8, if not before, he became subject to singular half-waking dreams. He fancied himself seated on the floor among several adult and naked sailors, whose genitals and buttocks he contemplated and handled with relish. He called himself the 'dirty pig' of these men, and felt that they were in some way his masters, ordering him to do uncleanly services to their bodies.[15]

Both his extreme youth and his low position suggest that this is a fantasy about being a bottom. The case history omits any reference to Bristol, yet the anonymity allows for more explictness. The egality and camaraderie of the first scene gives way to a scenario of sexual subservience in the second, A (the pseudonym chosen by Symonds[16]) submitting to the self-appellation of 'dirty pig' and obeying orders from the sailors to handle and service their genitals and buttocks from a crouched position between their thighs. The more detailed account is only possible, Kostenbaum concludes, once Symonds had given up his signature.[17]

Phyllis Grosskurth, in her introduction to the *Memoirs*, comments on the book's "curious admixture of candour and evasiveness", calling it "a hybrid, falling somewhere between literature and a psychological case history", and wondering why, if he were writing primarily for himself – or for posterity – he could not be entirely frank.[18] She sees a contradiction between Symonds' repeated insistence that the initial impetus for the *Memoirs* was a desire "to help others as unfortunate as himself", and her own observation that "the frequency with which he uses the words 'abnormal', 'morbid', 'unwholesome' suggests a growing suspicion that he might be some kind of monster." Symonds himself talks of "the strain of this attraction and repulsion – the intol-

---

15 Havelock Ellis and J.S. Symonds, *Sexual Inversion,* Wilson and Macmillan, 1897. Reprinted by Arno Press, 1975, 58.
16 After Symonds' death, Ellis used the pseudonym Z for Symonds' contribution to *Sexual Inversion,* thus demoting him from the primary letter of the alphabet to the ultimate letter. For a detailed account of their collaboration, see Kostenbaum, *Double Talk,* 43–67.
17 Ibid., 59.
18 Grosskurth, Introduction to M, 17; 28.

erable desire and the repudiation of mere fleshly satisfaction" (M, 274), the war between "a beauteous angel" and "a devil abhorred" (M, 283). Indeed, the two positions seem to characterize reverse discourse: Carpenter's perverse ruins and beautiful flowers; Proust's belief in the "sometimes beautiful, often hideous" accursed race; and Gide's debauched sodomites and honorable pederasts. The afflictions of a homophobic culture wrestle with the exalted sentiments of homosexual love. It is specifically this repeatability of statements that Foucault recognizes as constituting discourse and defining "*the possibilities of reinscription and transcription* (but also thresholds and limits), rather than limited and perishable individualities".[19] The relationships between these texts and their contribution to a mapping out of knowledge become clearer. A truth is emerging.

Prick to Prick, So Sweet

Although he recognized his desire for other men at an early age, Symonds repressed those feelings and tried to live a 'normal' life according to Victorian morals and social mores.[20] This involved marriage, at the age of twenty four, when he was, he claims, "still unconscious" of the sensuality of his desires for boys, although he was capable of romanticizing about them quite easily. His marriage, he hoped, would "satisfy the side of [his] nature which thrilled so strangely when [he] touched a boy" (M, 184). Yet within fifteen months of marriage his desires, still unsatisfied, threatened the tranquility he sought.

One episode Symonds recounts from this period described some graffito which deeply troubled him. Two cocks, pressed together, crudely scrawled on a slate: "an emphatic diagram of phallic meeting, glued together, gushing". By it, the words 'Prick to prick, so sweet' (M, 187). This phallic imagery was of "so *penetrative* a character […] that it pierced the very marrow" (emphasis added) of his soul. It became for Symonds a defining mo-

---

19 Michel Foucault, *The Archaeology of Knowledge,* trans. A. M. Sheridan Smith, Harper Colophon, 1972, 103.
20 See Jeffrey Weeks, *Sex, Politics and Society: The Regulation of Sexuality Since 1800,* Longman, 1981, chapter two.

ment in the discovery of his sexuality, a recognition, however crudely represented, of what he most desired: "That obscene graffito was the sign and symbol of a paramount and permanent craving of my physical and psychical nature" (M, 188). This sign and symbol pornographically condenses the distress of a desire hegemonically invalidated.

In the *Memoirs,* this revelation is succeeded by the birth of his first daughter, the fruit, not of prick to prick, but, to remain in the vernacular, prick to cunt. This would seem to foreground the sterility of the male–male union, to render that graffiti a cipher, a zero: two gushing pricks cannot procreate. Their sterility is further corroborated by the fact that at that time Symonds was only mentally investing in homosexual imagery and not physically acting on those impulses; a behaviour which, in the light of his procreative signifier (a child) would define his identity as heterosexual, not homosexual: his homosexual identity would appear to amount to zero. In thought, not deed. Which begs the question: where does identity come into being? Is it on the psychological or the physical plane? Is it constituted by desires or the acting out of those desires? Moreover, does the physical have less bearing on discursive reality than the physical, the material than the enunciative?

Foucault's analysis of sexuality focuses on the discursive impulse to distil every facet of human personality down to the existence of a true, essential and *pre*discursive sexuality, with the result that, for the homosexual:

> nothing that went into his total composition was unaffected by his sexuality. It was everywhere present in him: at the root of all his actions because it was their insidious and indefinitely active principle; written immodestly on his face and body because it was a secret that always gave itself away.[21]

An 'open secret', no less. In *A Problem in Modern Ethics,* Symonds criticizes the physiognomy argument, which saw in the

---

21 Foucault, *The History of Sexuality,* 1.43.

body of the homosexual unmistakeable signs of his deviant desire; in the *Memoirs* he colludes with it, confirming Foucault's argument by believing that his entire personality and ability to function as a writer and a thinker were detrimentally affected by his homosexuality: "It cannot be doubted that the congenital aberration of the passions which I have described has been the poison of my life." He refers to the time and energy wasted on expressing it, and how it has "interfered with the pursuit of study", how his marriage "has been spoiled by it" (M, 190).

Symonds carries within him "the seeds of what I know to be an incurable malady", a "deeply rooted perversion of the sexual instincts (uncontrollable, ineradicable, amounting to a monomania) to expose which in its relation to *my whole nature* has been the principle object of these memoirs (M, 281, emphasis added). He gives this "uncontrollable" sexual instinct a name: "the wolf", defined as "that undefined craving coloured with a vague but poignant hankering after males" (M, 187).

Upon viewing the prick-to-prick graffiti, "the wolf leapt out: my malaise of the moment was converted into a clairvoyant and tyrannical appetite for the thing which I had rejected five months earlier in the alley by the barracks" (i.e., sex with a grenadier). With this realization comes a clearer definition of that "vague but poignant hankering after males". Yet that vague hankering is experienced as "a precise hunger after sensual pleasure, whereof I had not dreamed before save in repulsive visions of the night" (M, 188).

As with Freud's Wolf-Man,[22] a 'deviant' sexuality is linked with a wolf, a wild and predatory carnivore, and an animal closely linked in folklore with unimaginable and unconscious fears. Symonds anthropomorphizes his homosexual desire as brutal and savage, something that preys on the precariously maintained stability of his heterosexual marriage. Symonds' 'civilised' self is at the mercy of a primitive and untamed sexual self which lies in waiting, ready to leap out in moments of

---

22 See M. Gardiner, *The Wolf-Man and Sigmund Freud*, Penguin, 1973.

weakness to "wreck [his] happiness and disturb [his] studious habits" (M, 187).

In a letter Edmund Gosse wrote to Symonds in 1890, where Gosse confesses to his own struggle with homosexual feelings, a similar anthropomorphism occurs:

> I know all that you speak of – the solitude, the rebellion, the despair... Years ago, I wanted to write to you about all this, and withdrew through cowardice. I have had a very fortunate life, but there has always been this obstinate twist in it. I have reached a quieter time – some beginnings of that Sophoclean period when the wild beast dies. He is not dead, but tamer; I understand him and the trick of his claws.[23]

Like Symonds, Gosse sees his desire as something separate from and in conflict with the civilized self, a wild beast in need of restraint, something of which he is at the mercy. It is the homosexual's life mission to "understand him and the trick of his claws."

The wolf would appear to be a potent and popular image in connection with homosexual desire. Proust, for example, when discussing the futility of a Sodomitic movement, or a city of Sodom, because no one would be seen dead in it, reasons that "they would repair to Sodom only on days of supreme necessity, when their own town was empty, at those seasons when hunger drives the wolf from the woods" (SG, 37). Homosexual desire is clearly a force to be reckoned with. When it craves fulfillment, there's no denying it. Symonds commits himself strongly to the belief that his desire for males is instinctual and innate, and believes that his attempt at redirecting it towards his wife forced his 'true' instincts to reassert themselves all the more violently. He presents the image of a man at the mercy of a brutal force:

> God help me! I cried. I felt humiliated, frightened, gripped in the clutch of doom. Nothing remained but to parry, palliate, procrastinate. There was no hope of escape. And all the

---

23 Grosskurth, *A Biography*, 280–1.

while the demon ravished my imagination with 'the love of the impossible'... From this decisive moment forward to the end, my life had to fly on a broken wing, and my main ambition has been to constitute a working compromise (*M*, 188)

For Symonds, desire is a demon with fangs and claws with which one must compromise in order to survive, the cause of great anxiety: a rather post-modern concept of sexuality as something threatening to one's sense of self.[24] An intelligent, civilized man is reduced to blind panic – "gripped in the clutch of doom" – at the merest whiff of that demon, desire, the almost Gothic signified of 'the love of the impossible', or 'a love that dares not speak its name'. This is wildly at odds with Symonds' liberationist position in *Modern Ethics,* where it becomes simply a question of liberating the homosexual from the social and legal constraints on his true self. If he wasn't forced – by fear of vilification and imprisonment – to hide his desire, the homosexual, Symonds argued, would be a noble and socially useful person. The public perception of homosexuals as suspicious and delinquent people is merely the inevitable result of their position in a culture that refuses to allow them to express themselves, he claimed. If only society would get off our backs we would all be happy. This ignores the often disturbing, unsettling and threatening ways in which sexual desire – especially dissident desire – is experienced in terms of its destabilizing effect on our sense of coherence and equilibrium. In *Modern Ethics,* Symonds argues that social education is the answer to oppression; a popular myth of sexual liberationist discourse.[25]

The image of a man in torment would seem to contradict the more popular portrait of Symonds as a sexual pioneer at ease with his sexuality and fighting for greater tolerance. Is the best a homosexual can hope for "a working compromise" with a demonic, voracious sexual appetite over which he has no control? At best, a life flown "on a broken wing"? He was caught between wanting to emphasize the pain experienced by homosexuals in

---
24   See Bersani, 'Is the Rectum a Grave?'.
25   What Foucault calls the 'repressive hypothesis'. See *The History of Sexuality,* 1.17–35.

a homophobic culture, and wanting to expound a theory of homosexual desire as an innate, healthy and natural phenomenon. Although not necessarily mutually exclusive positions, the dilemma this created in Symonds resulted in a concept of identity as precariously contingent on oppression and the medicalization of teleologically conceived sex behaviour. Without the torture, the oppression, from which to struggle and forge a sense of self, could one attain the status of a coherent identity? Liberationist gay movements also claim that gay identity is heroically wrestled from an oppressive and life-denying discourse and maintained in the face of complete adversity,[26] a position Foucault criticizes by seeing sexuality as the product of a discourse contingent upon such notions. Grosskurth, in her biography of Symonds, presents "the problem" of Symonds' homosexuality as not only "the overwhelming obsession of Symonds' life", but also the "central fact about the man",[27] supporting Foucault's theory on the prediscursive claims of sexuality.

As Symonds' tortured self-oppression indicates, the construction of this discursive belief in a central, true sexuality acted as a powerful means of self-surveillance, policing every gesture, every thought, every appetite. The rigorous examination of oneself for signs of inversion found its apotheosis in Xavier Mayne's *The Intersexes* (1908), which contained a questionnaire for readers keen to discover whether they were "at all Uranian".[28] But as Koestenbaum points out, "the book's secret purpose was to stimulate them to self-knowledge",[29] a discursive reversal. Symonds' *Memoirs* – which Bristow calls "a polemic about the specific identity that attended his sexual habits"[30] – could have played a central part in these private recognition scenes, with its dramatization of one individual's sexual development and its emphasis on a teleological and tragic will to truth. Unfortunately, his rather vague instructions to Brown to put Symonds' family first in all matters concerning his publications meant the

---

26 See, for example, Weeks, *Coming Out*; Silverstolpe, 'Benkert Was Not a Doctor'.
27 Grosskurth, *A Biography*, 262.
28 Mayne *The Intersexes*, 621.
29 Koestenbaum, *Double Talk*, 55.
30 Bristow, *Effeminate England*, 129.

manuscript didn't see the light of day for nearly a century, thus rendering the *Memoirs* nothing more than a marginally interesting historical document.

Writing in the Margins
Unlike the *Memoirs,* however, Symonds' privately printed essay *A Problem in Modern Ethics* (1891), which both Grosskurth and Weeks see as a counterpart to the *Memoirs,* circulated within the early 1890s homosexual underground, and was undoubtedly a signal text in the emergence of a coherent sense of the homosexual as a particular type of person/ality. Only fifty copies of the book were printed and despite the appearance on the title page of the disclaimer, 'Addressed especially to medical psychologists and jurists', it appears to have been sent out mainly to fellow inverts.

Grosskurth testifies that Symonds received hundreds of letters from men who saw within its pages a mirror image of their own feelings; men whose lives were equally characterized by constant conflict and furtiveness. For the first time, men whose sexual interest was predominantly, if not exclusively, in other men, could read about themselves in a way that did not classify their desires as a sin or a sickness. The margins of *Modern Ethics* were wide in order that recipients could return their copies with written comments, thus reversing the discourse and giving homosexuals themselves a vehicle to speak out via this pseudo-scientific text, or, as Koestenbaum argues, making readers into collaborators.[31] In this way, Symonds hoped to open up the debate to include inverts.

A tension is thus created between this desire to include the voice of inverts and Symonds' desire to collaborate with a man of science to lend authority to his voice, and highlights the comment made in chapter three about the absence of homosexual doctors speaking out on the subject. It was left to literary men to wrestle from medical discourse the authority with which to speak out. But that voice must constantly refer back to medi-

---
31 Koestenbaum, *Double Talk,* 55.

cal authority; as Koestenbaum comments, "The spectre of a homosexual doctor [...] dissolves contraries."[32] Subjectivity, oddly enough, is not seen as an authority. So-called medical objectivity is the only discourse allowed a voice. As Gosse's words testify: "The position of a young person so tormented is really that of a man buried alive and conscious, but *deprived of speech*"[33] (my emphasis). This tension between objectivity and subjectivity was one way through which a homosexual discourse was created, producing the concept of a gay identity as something negotiated between medical prescription and free self-inscription – a battle between the subject and a society concerned with objectifying him. The medical categorization made identification possible, but it supplied a rigid and narrow paradigm in which such identification could occur. Science was the only position from which one could speak with impunity and without imputation.[34] All religions require articles of faith and bearers of authority and medical science was rapidly becoming a new religion.

Yet by "describing homosexuality from a position within the subject, and then denying that one has entered the subject and made it one's own", imputation constantly threatens to cast a shadow over the speaker, resulting in what Koestenbaum calls "duplicitous double talk".[35] Medical authority on such an anxious subject is thus constantly threatened by the accusation that too much knowledge hints at personal experience.

In *Modern Ethics,* Symonds dismantles various medical theories – Moreau, Krafft-Ebing and Lombroso – and argues that medicine's focus on morbidity (as pathology) as a cause or condition of homosexuality is wide of the mark. He argues that morbidity is, rather, the *result* of living in a society which legislates against and culturally prohibits homosexuality:

---

32 Ibid., 62.
33 Quoted in Grosskurth, *A Biography,* 282.
34 Havelock Ellis' concerns about writing on homosexuality were alleviated by a lecturer on insanity at the Westminster Hospital, who wrote: "so long as you confine your appeal to the jurist, the alienist and the scientific reader, no shadow of imputation ought to rest upon you". Quoted in Havelock Ellis, *A Note on the Bedborough Trial* [1898], D.C. McMurtie, 1925.
35 Kostenbaum, *Double Talk,* 61.

> The grain of truth contained in this vulgar error is that, under the prevalent laws and hostilities of modern society, the inverted passion has to be indulged furtively, spasmodically, hysterically; that the repression of it through fear and shame frequently leads to habits of self-abuse; and that its unconquerable solicitations sometimes convert it from a healthy outlet of the sexual nature into a morbid monomania.[36]

Although we may find it easy to criticize this in the light of recent work such as that of Foucault, Symonds was, with such an approach, positing homosexual desire as a perfectly natural drive, not as the debauched behaviour of bored libertines or frustrated prisoners. For Symonds, homosexual desire was inborn and therefore natural, and "there is no proof that they are the subjects of disease".[37]

Symonds' main concern in *Modern Ethics* was to disassociate homosexuality from the morbidity/pathology model, a link established by medical writers such as Krafft-Ebing and Tardieu. Using Ulrichs' theories enabled Symonds to root a discussion on homosexuality within a scientific paradigm without recourse to contemporary theories of morbidity or degeneration. Unfortunately, the appropriation of Ulrichs' formula for arguing the biological naturalism of same-sex desire imported at the same time a theory of homosexuality based, first and foremost, on gender inversion. The homosexual as constructed within medical discourse was thereby violently at odds with traditional masculinity. In this way, sexual transgression became gender transgression, and *vice versa*.

By his daily correspondence with Ulrichs, who by now lived in Italy, and his inclusion of Ulrichs' theories in *Modern Ethics*, Symonds acted as the portal through which the inversion trope passed into the consciousness of homosexual Britons. Along with the *Memoirs* and his earlier pamphlet, *A Problem in Greek Ethics*, it can be counted "among the first modern documents to emphasize how human identity must primarily be under-

---

36 Symonds, *Modern Ethics*, 13.
37 Ibid., 128.

stood in terms of sexual preference".[38] At the same time, Wilde's *A Picture of Dorian Gray*[39] was establishing a literary mirror in which many homosexuals recognized a way of being which refuted traditional masculinity and presented one conduit – arguably, the only visible and culturally permissible identity at that time – through which male–male love could be articulated. In the absence of visible alternatives, the inversion trope became the central trope for homosexuality.

The Aversa Venus

Like Gide and Carpenter, Symonds relied on the Greek model of pederasty in his defense of male–male love, whilst at the same time denying that anal sex played any significant role in homosexual relations. Did the anus function as a site of pleasure between men at the time these writers lived? Was its absence in apologies such as those by Gide and Carpenter a deliberate avoidance of a delicate subject? Or was it, rather, a minority taste within a minority taste? And what do the answers to these questions tell us about the symbolic and cultural role of that much-maligned orifice? In *Modern Ethics,* Symonds writes:

> It is the common belief that one, and only one, unmentionable act is what the lovers seek as the source of their unnatural gratification, and that this produces spinal disease, epilepsy, consumption, dropsy, and the like. Nothing can be more mistaken, as the scientifically reported cases of avowed and adult sinners demonstrate. Neither do they invariably or even usually prefer the *aversa Venus*; nor, when this happens, do they exhibit peculiar signs of suffering in health.[40]

---

38 Bristow, *Effeminate England,* 131.

39 After reading Wilde's novel, Symonds wrote to a friend that he thought the book "odd and very audacious", "unwholesome in tone", but nonetheless "artistically and psychologically interesting", supporting the view of this thesis that a dialectic existed between medical and literary discourses. Quoted in H. M. Hyde, *Oscar Wilde,* Eyre Methuen, 1976, 185.

40 Symonds, *Modern Ethics,* 12–13.

In the process of denying this "unmentionable act" Symonds finds himself paradoxically defending it as not detrimental to individual health. His position is further complicated when, discussing Mantegazza's theory that 'anomalous passions' can be explained by a misdirection of nerves from the penis to the rectum, he writes "that an intimate connection exists between the nerves of the reproduction organs and the nerves of the rectum is known to anatomists and is felt by everybody".[41] That "felt by everybody" cunningly universalizes rectal pleasure and shifts the topic away from homosexuality.

Given the stringent anti-buggery laws in place at the time he was writing, it is hardly surprising that the majority of case studies in *Sexual Inversion,* for example, make no mention of it. As Ellis comments:

> It will be observed that in the preceding ten cases little reference is made to the practice of *paedicatio* or *immissio penis in anum*. It is probable that in none of these cases […] has it been practiced. In the two following cases it has occasionally been practiced, but only with repugnance and not as the satisfaction of an instinct.[42]

Anal intercourse is clearly considered not to be instinctual to the homosexual. If performed, it would appear to inspire repugnance, not pleasure (recall Gide's horror at viewing a scene of sodomy in chapter one). Symonds' most potent symbol of homosexual desire – "prick to prick" – erases the anus and establishes the sameness of male–male eroticism in purely phallic terms. By foregrounding the phallus and downplaying the anus, rejecting sodomy as the behaviour of effeminate degenerates, Symonds maintains a strong link between sodomy and effeminacy. Masculinity and passive anal sex thus become mutually exclusive phenomena, and effeminacy becomes the 'natural' and inevitable behaviour of the passive homosexual. To be anally re-

---
41 Ibid., 81.
42 Ellis and Symonds, *Sexual Inversion,* 51.

ceptive inevitably emasculates a man within a dimorphic gender system.

Recalling the Wolf-Man's primal scene, which for Freud was witnessing his parents performing *coitus a tergo,* or from behind, Symonds' fear of 'the wolf' can be read as a fear of sodomy, a fear of the gay anus. Just as the Wolf-Man fears the castration which is the inevitable outcome of allowing the father to penetrate him – a 'truth' confirmed by seeing his mother's lack of a phallus – so too Symonds fears the lycanthropic bestiality[43] of sodomy and its concommitent emasculation and effeminization. Anal sex becomes the true *l'amour de l'impossible,* the thing that terrified not only Symonds but also Gide, Carpenter and Proust. That is not to say that all four men desired to get fucked, but the reiteration of that fear inscribes itself on the surface of homosexual discourse and a deep shame becomes attached to the act itself. It is an act to be avoided, not only for fear of effeminacy but also, and more importantly, for fear of confirming the heterosexual hegemony's worst fears: that all homosexuals are passive sodomites.

The stylistics of existence ascribed to by these four writers foregrounds comradeship, love, affection, and demonizes physical indulgence, as if these things could not possibly co-exist. Symonds wants no more than "the blameless proximity of [a] pure person" (M, 266). (He found peace and tranquility in the last years of his life in a remote part of the Swiss Alps, living in the shadow of a mountain named, ironically, Wolfgang).

The heterological assumption that desire springs from lack demands that sexual receptivity in a man confirms his lack of 'real' manhood. Whilst the locker room warning to 'mind yer backs' ascribes the active role to the assumed homosexual, *at the same time* it addresses the real fear that desire for anal sex is contagious, that submitting in this way to another male will

---

43 See Alan Bray, *Homosexuality in Renaissance Britain*, Gay Men's Press, 1982, for a discussion of the signifying potential of homosexuality through mythic association with lycanthropes, or werewolves, in the early modern period.

rob one of one's masculinity. Homophobic discourse is nothing if not contradictory.[44]

One thing that fascinated Symonds was the idea that the absorption of semen could masculinize. Whilst he cites experiments by Silvio Ventuir in which semen was injected into patients, one can't help also conjuring up oral and anal sex as conduits for this 'injection': the receptive partner, rather than having his masculinity robbed, has it supplemented within such logic. The discursive impossibility of such logic should be clear from my readings of these four writers' work and I would like, in the following conclusion, to explore not only the relations between the four texts and their formulation of a specific discourse based on shared 'truths', but also to rehearse provocatively ways in which the discourse mapped out by them might be reversed in the interests of the 'butch bottom'. How might the stigma attached to getting fucked be overcome, the ghost of Ulrichs finally exorcised?

---

[44] See Halperin, *Saint Foucault*, 33–8.

Conclusion

Fear of a Gay Anus

> *"Ah, did you but know how delicate is one's enjoyment when a heavy prick fills the behind...No, no, in the wide world there is no pleasure to rival this one; it is the delight of philosophers, that of heroes, it would be that of the gods were not the parts used in this divine conjugation the only gods we on earth should reverence!"*
> – Marquis de Sade, *Philosophy in the Bedroom*

> *"The purpose of history, guided by genealogy, is not to discover the roots of our identity but to commit ourselves to its dissipation."*
> – Michel Foucault, 'Nietzsche, Genealogy, History'

What are the relations between the statements made by these four writers? How do they formulate a body of knowledge, a discourse? What are the referents, the correlations, the themes?[1] How is meaning established at the level of discourse? How does that discourse become solid? What are its limits? How does it let us down? And how can we change it?

As these readings have shown, these four writers signal a deep anxiety about the body and its pleasures. Such isomorphism constitutes a discursivity lacking in materiality. Whilst the task of much late twentieth century theory such as Golding, Haver and Butler has been to "bring the body out from the shadow of the mind, bring practice out from the shadow of theory",[2] it would appear that a century ago homosexual discourse actively directed attention away from the body and onto a mastery over the body. The 'homosexual body' as a discursive entity was for-

---
1 Foucault, *The Archaeology of Knowledge*, 21–30.
2 Michael Hardt quoted in Golding, *The Eight Technologies of Otherness*, 277.

mulated on the subordination of the body as a material entity with dangerous orifices and dark desires.

In this way, these texts help towards demarcating the limits of that discourse. By adopting medical theories and terminology, these four writers didn't so much reverse discourse as supply it with experiential data. However much the identity politics instigated by these texts exceeded the medical categorization and subjectivation, by working within the same theoretical field they ultimately consolidated the binarisms immanent in the normative theories of desire with which they worked. The heterological nature of those theories limited the 'truth' which could emerge. In this sense, one can say that there is no reverse discourse: there is only discourse. The field of knowledge to which these four texts responded and contributed was one and the same. Their resistence was also a capitulation. Neither Gide, nor Proust, nor Carpenter or Symonds formulated a truly *homo*sexual theory of desire as desire for the same. Their texts are no cartography of a homotopia.

The theories of desire developed within Western epistemology are predicated on concepts of complementarity developed out of the male/female binary, which is embedded within a normativising and naturalizing scientific discourse. These theories understand desire within a register of lack, or difference, which is incapable of addressing a desire for the same; a homosexual desire. Within them, same-sex desire is never more than a double helix with no obvious or 'natural' complementarity. The attempt to force the square peg of same-sex desire into the round hole of the male/female binary has resulted in a skewed understanding of homosexuality as a mimesis of heterosexuality, in which 'male' and 'female' roles are adopted to overcome this absence of complementarity. Formulated within a heterosexual hegemony, or heterology, the theories of desire available, from sexology through to Freudianism and Lacanianism, all work within a rubric of sexual difference: Freud's 'heterosexual dispositions'; Lacan's 'Having and Being the Phallus'. These theories deny homosexuality. We cannot use them. To use them is to heterosexualize homosexuality.

The heterosexualization occurs through the installation of the normative heterosexual male/female dyad, underpinned by a naturalizing discourse on procreation. As the four texts demonstrate, a refusal to entertain the possibility of anal pleasure became a central tenet of the emancipationist programme. One could say the anus is the gaping void in homosexual discourse, the absence of which bears witness to an anxiety about its very existence. As I have shown, this anxiety is due to the feminization attached to the so-called passive role; and this is due to the heterosexual model of desire upon which the homosexual model was predicated. Even the refusal to talk about anal sex marks it as the secret and puts it at the heart of homosexual discourse. For at the level of discourse, the accordance of a value or truth can derive not only from what is said, "but also what it speaks of, its theme",[3] which can derive from what is not said as much as from what is said. To mention anal sex drew suspicion that one was a passive sodomite. Like the self-consuming snake Ourobouris, this chain of associations is circuitous, feeding into itself endlessly: homosexuality = anal passivity = effeminacy = homosexuality...

By failing to challenge these associations, Gide, Proust, Carpenter and Symonds – however pioneering – installed them, and all their concomitant anxieties, within the modern discourse on 'gay identity'. Through their uncritical adoption as *Urtexts* of homosexual discourse, these writings formed a significant part of the foundations upon which our current understandings of homosexual identity were built. In this sense, this book has been driven by the exigencies of a wider, more contemporary political programme: an attempt to redefine the homosexual/homosexuality. This redefinition is predicated on the notion of sameness as opposed to difference. Sex between two men – or, more specifically, intercourse – should not be seen as a mimetic gesture of heterosexual intercourse. The desire to make such a reading stems, I have tried to show, from a long-standing tradition of binary thinking within metaphysics, science, sociology, and an-

---

3 Foucault, *The Archaeology of Knowledge*, 90.

thropology. But within this formulation, as we saw in Proust, there was no such thing as a homosexual.

Fundamental Pleasures

The only nineteenth century writer to acknowledge sodomy in remotely positive terms was Sir Richard Burton, whose 1885 'Terminal Essay' explained the phenomenon as occurring within what he referred to as the Sotadic Zone, a geographical area significantly excluding Western Europe. Anal intercourse could be granted discursive existence only on the understanding that it was the barbaric behaviour of uncivilized Easterners, figures constructed as the Other, upon whom all forms of debauchery could be safely projected. Further distance was achieved by the declaration that "it is a medical question whose discussion would be out of place here".[4] No attempts at pseudo-science here. Burton further obscures his source material by quoting it in Latin, Greek and German, and putting certain less palatable phrases in French. As Rudi Bleys points out, Burton "held onto a pre-modern notion of sodomy as an act".[5] Yet, for Burton, too, same-sex activity was predicated on "a blending of the feminine and the masculine".[6] Gender would appear to be inextricably linked with sexuality from the very beginnings of our understandings of both.

Through the lens of nineteenth century sexology, only passive sodomites were innate homosexuals – and innate homosexuality was recognizable through a salient and reviled effeminacy. The active partner's reasons for indulging in such behaviour were considered to be more varied and contingent (lack of women, general debauchery, too much masturbation, curiosity, money, etc). Sexology's construction of innate homosexuality as a discrete category indiscreetly recognizable by atypical gender behaviour served a need to promote homosexuals as visibly different from heterosexuals at a time when gender roles were

---

[4] Richard Burton, 'Terminal Essay', in *The Thousand Nights and a Night* [1850], Heritage Press, New Tork, 1962, vols 5 & 6, 3749.

[5] Bleys, *Geography of Perversion*, 216

[6] Burton, 'Terminal Essay', 3750.

undergoing great change and as such were the site of enormous cultural anxiety. Moreover, this visible difference spoke of an essential interior difference which constituted human sexuality along two separate axes: heterosexuality and homosexuality; one prescribed the other proscribed. As such, homosexuality in its visibly different form – effeminacy – is far more palatable to a culture dependent upon the stability of heterosexual norms. Indeed, that stability is contingent upon the construction of homosexuals as Other, as a race apart, against which normative heterosexual identities can be formulated. Male passivity threatens to destabilize the construction of masculine identity as active, so much that males who are passive cannot be seen as men, they have relinquished their male privilege, and occupy the site of perversion and emasculation. Conversely, if one only ever adopts the active role, one can, in a sense, avoid the proscriptive taint of being 'less of a man'; one is seen as using another man 'as if he were a woman'.

Moe Meyer's work on the politics of posing in regard to Wilde's production of the 'homosexual' as a discursive figure is useful in revealing how surface and depth are read against each other in the construction of an interiority made comprehensible by an identifiable exteriority.[7] Edelman, too, explores the ways in which discourse has posited that the 'homosexual' carries on the surface of his body the indelible and horrifically decipherable marks of his essential deviance. This inscription is necessary, he concludes, to mark homosexual men as different from heterosexual men, given that, in reality, such difference is not visible but construed.[8] Coining a neologism – homographesis – from the two words homograph and graphesis, Edelman argues that the visibly different homosexual body was an inscribed figure, a discursive entity, whose difference was written on the surface of the body. A homograph is a word identical in spelling but different in meaning: the homosexual male body must be given a different meaning to that of the heterosexual male body,

---

7   Moe Meyer, 'Under the Sign of Wilde: An Archeology of Posing', in *Id.* (ed.), *The Politics and Poetics of Camp*, Routledge, 1994.
8   Edelman, *Homographesis*, 10.

given that on the surface such differences need not be apparent. The discursive inscription upon the homosexual body of differences always apparent was the most (homo)graphic way of signaling such difference.[9] So while masculinity was inscribed on the surface of the heterosexual male body as the indelible mark of his identity, femininity became graphically, elaborately, inscribed on the surface of the homosexual male body as the indelible mark of identity. And that femininity carried with it all the charge of passivity, receptivity, an ability to be endlessly penetrated, and as such to be, horrifically, the site of disease – both culturally and literally. Bersani points out the ways in which

> the realities of syphilis in the nineteenth century and of AIDS today legitimate a fantasy of female sexuality as intrinsically diseased; and promiscuity in this fantasy, far from merely increasing the risk of infection, is the *sign of infection*. Women and gay men spread their legs with an unquenchable appetite for destruction.[10]

This conflation of female sexuality and gay male sexuality around a trope of receptivity is most graphically exemplified by the terms man-cunt and boy-pussy. To use the anus to receive an erect penis feminizes not only that orifice, metamorphosing it into a vagina, but also, as the closed, private and impenetrable site of masculine identity, this usage threatens, moreover, to feminize the entire body, the identity itself.

The Politics and Poetics of the Anus

In contrast to the blanket denial of anal sex by the four authors presented here, homosexual pornography from the late nineteenth century presents it as a common activity. In *Teleny,* for example, one character asks rhetorically, "Ah!... what pleasures can be compared with those of the Cities of the Plain?"[11] The

---
9   Ibid.
10 Bersani, 'Is the Rectum a Grave?', 211. Original emphasis. Further citations will appear in brackets indicated by the abbreviation RG.
11 Anon., *Teleny* [1884], Gay Sunshine Press, 1984, 140.

Sins of the Cities of the Plain is the title of another late Victorian homosexual porn novel, in which the narrator, Jack Saul, recounts his sexual history as both active and passive partner. No sign here of that repugnance referred to by Ellis. Rather, a lewd, crude celebration of sodomy, a paean to paedicatio. Indeed, the title of one chapter, 'Same Old Story: Arses Preferred to Cunts',[12] would seem to foreground the anus as the favoured site of pleasure-taking (albeit the active partner's pleasure is the main concern in such a statement).

It would seem, then, that an openness about anal sex was only available in exchange for anonymity, in the way that Symonds' sexual explicitness was possible only upon abdicating his signature. Privately printed and secretly circulated, pornography – anonymous or pseudonomous – was able to represent explicitly what even medical texts often shied away from discussing and apologist accounts denied.

The anus as the site of particular anxiety, a discursive battleground in the field of sexuality, is a point elaborated on by 1970s gay theorists Guy Hocquenghem and Mario Mieli, for whom it was a revolutionary orifice. Now wildly outdated and discreted for their naïve utopianism, it will nevertheless be beneficial to explore briefly their 'anal politics' as their work indicates that the anxieties surrounding anal sex are still in place in the late twentieth century – due, I believe, in part at least, to the normative binarisms underpinning the definition of homosexuality.

Hocquenghem claims, "whereas the phallus is essentially social, the anus is essentially private",[13] which could explain its more revered place in privately printed pornography. Hocquenghem follows Freud in seeing "the anal stage as the stage of formation of the person" (HD, 96), an organ whose only function is private. Unlike the phallus, the anus does not enjoy a social role as an object of desire or admiration; any desire directed towards the anus must be sublimated to maintain

---

12 Anon., *The Sins of the Cities of the Plain; or the Recollections of a Mary-Ann with short essays on Sodomy and Tribadism* [1881], Masquerade Bad Boy Books, 1992.
13 Guy Hocquenghem, *Homosexual Desire,* trans. Daniella Dangoor, Duke University Press, 1993, 96. Further citations will appear in brackets, indicated by the abbreviation HD.

not only the organization of society around the great signifier, but also a stable sense of self. This is because "ours is a phallic society, and the quantity of possible pleasure is determined in relation to the phallus" (*HD*, 95). For this reason, Hocquenghem argues that the homosexual use of the anus as a pleasure-giving organ challenges the anality-sublimation by restoring its desiring use. This desiring use exists in everyone, he believes, but its sublimation is a prerequisite of the socialization process and the formation of the subject. As such, homosexual desire can be seen as essentially anti-social, for "homosexuality primarily means anal homosexuality, sodomy" (*HD*, 98). For him, sociality itself is contingent on the sublimation of the erotic value of the anus. Furthermore, a desublimation of this desiring use of the anus can lead to a loss – or shattering – of identity. Bersani sees this as a positive challenge to monolithic sexuality: "*To be penetrated is to abdicate power*" (*RG*, 212, original emphasis), and that abdication of power is, ultimately, a challenge to traditional masculinity. Bersani believes that "the value of powerlessness in both men and women" has been denied, by which he means not passivity or gentleness, but "a more radical disintegration and humiliation of the self" (*RG*, 217). This disintegration of the self is the real threat of homosexuality, argues Bersani, and it is inextricably linked to the terrifying and seductive image of "a grown man, legs high in the air, unable to refuse the suicidal ecstasy of being a woman" (*RG*, 212). He links passive sodomy to the sexual politics of power, which places gay men in the same position as heterosexual women: on the receiving end of that inviolate symbol of mastery, the Phallus. Once again, heterological thinking is governing the readings of sexual positions and the sameness of homosexual intercourse is conflated with the difference of heterosexual intercourse.

The obvious anatomical point of departure for this analogy between gay men and straight women is that the former also possess a phallus, that signifier whose lack is supposed to be the predicate of their desire. The anus exists as a separate erotic site and intercourse between men, therefore, should not be seen as a displaced heterosexuality which renders the receptive partner female, but, on the contrary, a purely *homo*sexual act – i.e., a sexual act between two bodies which are the *same* sex.

In these accounts, anal sex becomes the diacritical marker distinguishing gay sexuality. Whilst Hocquenghem prefers to emphasise the psychological and political aspects, at the expense of any concept of pleasure, Mieli, on the other hand, bluntly states:

> The point is, that if you get fucked, if you know what tremendous enjoyment is to be had from anal intercourse, then you necessarily become different from the 'normal' run of people with a frigid arse. You know yourself more deeply.[14]

For Mieli, being penetrated heightens one's sense of self rather than, as Bersani suggests, threatening to shatter it. To get fucked gives one greater knowledge of who one is: *You know yourself more deeply.* It becomes the key lesson in a heuristics of pleasure. But one which produces enormous anxiety. Mieli isolates anal sex as the one aspect of homosexuality that heterosexual men fear above all: "This is undoubtedly due not just to the repression of their anal desire, but also to their fear of castration – in essence, the fear of falling off the masculine pedestal into the 'female' role" (*HL,* 139). However, he then states that every male experiences a fear of castration, without making it clear whether this includes those men who enjoy being penetrated. The problem, once again, is the conflation of the anus with the vagina.[15] Why is it not possible for a man to be penetrated without automatically and inevitably falling "into the 'female' role"? Mieli suggests that the fear of falling into this role, which is linked to the fear of losing one's virility, is really a fear of the loss of identity. It would seem that a penetration is being perpetrated not only on an orifice but on identity itelf: the skin as identity boundary.

---

14 Mario Mieli, *Homosexuality and Liberation: Elements of a Gay Critique,* trans. David Fernbach, Gay Men's Press, 1980, 139. Further citations will appear in brackets indicated by the abbreviation *HL.*

15 Charles Socarides, a renowned homophobe, accused any psychoanalyst who attempted to help a homosexual of elevating the anus to the status of the vagina.

For Hocquenghem too the homosexual role is a confused identity – something they share with women. For homosexual men, this confusion arises from the fact that, given its private role in the formation of the self, "any social use of the anus [...]creates the risk of a loss of identity" (*HD*, 101). This loss can be equated to the powerlessness, the psychic disintegration of which Bersani speaks. Both Mieli and Hocquenghem root this anxiety in the psychic processes governing the creation of the subject within traditional psychoanalytic patterns, whereby the phallus is the marker for sexual differentiation and identity formation. Mieli argues that detached from this pattern, anal sex can be enjoyed for the simple physical pleasure it is, but that the precondition for this is a reciprocity in which both partners give and take. Liberation of the arsehole would seem to lead to a greater liberation of the individual. By linking anal repression to the rule of the phallus in patriarchal capitalism, Hocquenghem suggests a similar theory; as he playfully states in his essay 'Towards an Irrecuperable Pederasty', "Our assholes are revolutionary."[16] For this reason, their work has been largely discredited as working with what Foucault calls the 'repressive hypothesis'.

A correlation – we could even call it a binarism – emerges between the phallus and the anus, in which a reinvestment of the anus "collectively and libidinally would involve a proportional weakening of the great phallic signifier" (*HD*, 103). Our culture's fear of the gay anus begins to make sense when one considers that any libidinal use of it robs the phallus of its power as primary signifier. In this model, we could fuck our way to revolution. Yet, for Mieli at least, homosexuality remains a signifier of "the woman within", a form of "trans-sexuality", and 'masculinity' becomes something one relinquishes through the act of sodomy. Again, we see homosexuality and masculinity as irreconcilable polarities, occupying opposite sides of that wounding cut '/', which establishes them as opposing terms. Again, we come up against the need for a non-heterological – a homological? –

---

[16] Guy Hocquenghem, 'Towards an Irrecuperable Pederasty', trans. Chris Fox, in Jonathan Goldberg (ed.), *Reclaiming Sodom*, Routledge, 1993, 236.

definition of same-sex desire; one which refuses to perpetuate such myths.

The Butch Bottom

The problems facing the homosexual man trying to negotiate an identity between the two poles of overt effeminacy and traditional masculinity are obvious. Particularly today, when passing as straight is considered a cop-out while to be straight-acting is considered a turn-on.[17] This negotiation process is complicated further if one happens to enjoy getting fucked, a behaviour traditionally considered, as I have shown, to be demeaning, disempowering, and effeminizing. Even within homosexual subcultures, there is a strong belief that real men give, pansies take. The concept of the 'butch bottom' is almost culturally inconceivable, for the very act of allowing a man to penetrate one's body would seem to submit one to a necessary and unavoidable ontological femaleness within the normative binaries of active/passive and male/female.

When Foucault stated in an interview that "most gays feel the passive role is in some way demeaning"[18] he is referring explicitly to this knot of definitional axes. Passivity is seen as a non-male behaviour, for true maleness is predicated on activity. Foucault claims that "s&m has actually helped alleviate this problem somewhat".[19] The rules governing the giving and taking of pleasure/pain in the sm scenario empower the bottom: s/he is in control, regulating the pleasures/pains received. There is no inherent inferiority attached to the taking of pleasure. The femininity/inferiority association is a political manoeuvre governing the correct behaviour of men and women in patriarchal society. Semantically, we need to see the bottom as taking pleasure, not just giving it; to re-establish the equality between the two partners.

---

17 For a discussion of passing see Judith Butler, *Bodies That Matter: On the Discursive Limits of "Sex"*, Routledge, 1993, 167–85.
18 Foucault, *Foucault Live*, 227.
19 Ibid.

The *New Joy of Gay Sex* worryingly reinforces the passive aspect of being a bottom by stating that:

> Being a bottom is [...] more importantly a state of mind, a feeling one has about oneself in relationship to other men. 'Bottom' (in sexual terms) denotes wanting to be taken care of and to be directed by the 'top'. In some men it may reflect an important streak of passivity, as if to say, "I want to give myself up to you."[20]

This is essentialism of the worst kind, conflating a more or less universal need for care with a sexual preference. In some men, being a bottom may well coincide with wanting to give oneself up to another man, but it could also be the opposite. Or something else entirely. Wanting to get fucked needn't be symptomatic of wanting to be told what to do. It needn't be an abdication of autonomy. Assuming the desire and pleasure is mutual, the bottom is taking exactly what he wants and is very much in control of, the agent of, his own desires.[21] Even Bersani, in his analysis of gay appropriations of masculinity in the fashion for machismo, calls it a "mockery [...] based on the dark suspicion that you may not be getting the real article" (RG, 208), so ingrained is the belief that masculinity is completely at odds with homosexuality. 'Masculine/homosexual', as Dollimore states, is one of the most violently hierarchical of all binarism[22]; one which has been directly endorsed by the medical discourse and indirectly by the likes of Gide, Proust, Carpenter and Symonds.

---

20 Charles Silverstein and Felice Picano, *The New Joy of Gay Sex*, Gay Men's Press, 1993, 20.

21 This is where the imagined vast divide between SM practices and vanilla sex forecloses a mutual learning process. By exploring the top/bottom relationship in SM, it may be possible to learn something capable of application within a vanilla scenario: "The fact is, S&M is controlled and responsible sexual activity. We have a very highly developed sense of ethics. We have a golden rule that when the bottom [masochist] says enough, the activity stops." Quoted in Weeks, *Invented Moralities*, 128. In this scenario, the bottom does not want to be taken care of, nor abdicate autonomy. Rather, the bottom is in charge, determining the limits of the game, and not at the mercy of the top. Not powerless or abused.

22 Jonathan Dollimore, 'Homophobia and Sexual Difference', in *Sexual Difference*, Oxford Literary Review, 1986, 5.

Gide et al. downplayed sodomy's role in homosexual desire ostensibly because they associated it with effeminacy and degeneracy, but it also represents a form of male intimacy that is culturally too threatening. Within a heterosexual hegemony, sexual intimacy is the privilege of a heterosexual union. Gay anal sex is dangerous because it so closely resembles traditional heterosexual intercourse in terms of positionality that when the male/female pattern is mapped onto the male–male coupling, the insertee becomes a woman. To alter the perception, one must alter the definition, and see homosexuality as a sexuality in its own right, without recourse to an 'original' heterosexuality which is being aped, ineptly (due to anatomical differences). To recognize in homosexuality the potential to recalibrate desires and pleasures along non-binaric lines.

As Gide argued, pleasure, not procreation, is the motor for sexual activity. Libido is distinct from the desire to reproduce. In an age of birth control, much heterosexual activity is sterile, anyway, indulged in for pleasure. Because one act precedes the other, the two have been conflated, the 'naturalness' of the link used to support arguments for the 'unnaturalness' of non-procreative or recreative sex.

No system of thought currently exists that can contain *homos*. The belief that two sexes constitute difference plagues our world view. Our very thought processes have become two-tiered, binaric, like animals entering the ark. Difference is sought as a way of understanding our world. Male–male and female–female desire buckles this logic in a profound and underestimated way. The appropriation of gender inversion as the only explanation/representation of same-sexness, and the consolidation of this belief by homosexual writers such as Symonds et al., has damaged homosexuals for over a century, establishing homosexuality as antithetical to traditional gender roles. The responses against such a belief have attacked effeminacy in men and butchness in women; have been anti-female, misogynistic and homophobic. Yet, need this be the case? Effeminate or misogynistic? Active or passive? Doesn't homosexual desire offer an ideal opportunity to rethink the ways desire has been theorized within heterologic systems of thought?

If gender and sexual categories are historically constructed, and if the mechanisms of their emergence and maintenance can be understood, then they are open to transformation. This is something that has been instigated by the Queer movement, which has refused old categories and started working towards the theorization of new ways of seeing desire. This has meant not just challenging the category of sexuality, but also the "indescribably wide range of social institutions" in which "the logic of the sexual order is so deeply embedded by now".[23] The body has entered theory and introduced there all the chaos of desire. The old order is crumbling. It has become clear that something is lacking in 'lack'. And that something is the productive, creative, imaginative excess of bodies that matter. "We need a non-taxonomic method"; one that "can express queer desire as a desire that is different in kind rather than different in degreee from other manifestations of desire".[24]

By seeing the association of femininity and male homosexuality as a discursive and performative phenomenon in the service of a heterosexual/heterological hegemony, we can begin what Haver calls "a praxis of a poiesis, first and last erotic".[25] And this poiesis, this realizing "the object […] as the result produced by an always already fully accomplished subjectivity (or a subjectivity that will be accomplished in and through poiesis)",[26] is "a route, a mapping, an impossible geography – impossible not because it does not exist, but because it exists and does not exist exactly at the same time"[27]; what Golding calls the "otherside of otherness".[28]

---

23 Michael Warner, Introduction to *Id.* (ed.), *Fear of a Queer Planet: Queer Politics and Social Theory*, University of Minnesota Press, 1993, xiii.

24 Elspeth Probyn, 'Queer Belongings', in *Id.* and E. Grosz (eds), *Sexy Bodies: The Strange Carnalities of Feminism*, Routledge, 1995, 13.

25 William Haver, *The Body of This Death: Historicity and Sociality in the Time of AIDS*, Stanford University Press, 1996, 189.

26 Ibid.

27 Golding, 'Sexual Manners', 166.

28 Sue Golding, 'The Excess: An Added Remark on Sex, Rubber, Ethics, and Other Impurities', in *New Formations* 19: 'Perversity' (Spring 1993).

Foucault claimed that "a normalizing society is the historical outcome of a technology of power centred on life" (*HS*, 144). Centred on life because heterosexuality must be construed and promoted in terms of procreating life, leaving homosexuality to be set up in opposition to this; in opposition to life (AIDS has only reinforced this). This is because life, rather than pleasure, has been the focus of scientific attention. Pleasure cannot be quantified, measured, categorized by scientific enquiry; but life can. Therefore, the technology of power which has been the chief strategy of the medical profession for the last one hundred years has ignored pleasure. So much so that pleasure has been rendered as antithetical to life. Pleasure vs. Life. Coterminous with this was the capitalist demand for profitable production, whereby pleasure became antithetical to production as well as reproduction.[29] Foucault foregrounded pleasure over desire because a politics of pleasure would diminish the normalizing gaze of medical enquiry and destabilize the claim to rightness of heterosexuality. Desire has been used as a measure of pathology.[30]

As we approach the millennium, the time is ripe for a break from the old notions of desire. If the nominational shift from 'lesbian and gay' to 'queer' is to achieve anything, let it be a redefinition of same-sex desire that is not reliant on dominant fictions of what a sexual relationship should be; a definition that doesn't privilege difference over sameness, the (public) phallus over the (private) anus; one that recognizes in all its radical potentiality the reality of two bodies exchanging pleasure; a different economy of bodies and pleasures, as Foucault called for, which doesn't work within the violence hierarchy of binary male/female, characterized as it is – like all binarisms – by that deep cut[31] ('/') to which heterosexual doctors could not administer aid, but could only leave to fester, for a whole century. By refusing gender difference as the ground for the figuring of our desires, and instead foregrounding bodies and pleasures, we

---
29 Herbert Marcuse, *Eros and Civilisation: A Philosophical Inquiry into Freud*, Ark Paperbacks, 1987, esp. 255–61.
30 See Halperin, *Saint Foucault*, 93–7.
31 Golding, 'Curiosity', in *Id.* (ed.), *The Eight Technologies*, 16; 21.

could begin to equalize sexuality and work towards a true sexual democracy, a true Homotopia.

Bibliography

Primary texts

Carpenter, Edward, *Civilisation: Its Cause and Cure,* London: 1889.

———, *The Intermediate Sex,* London: George Allen & Unwin Ltd, 1908.

———, *Intermediate Types Among Primitive Folk,* London: George Allen & Unwin Ltd, 1914.

———, *My Days and Dreams,* London: Allen & Unwin, 1916.

———, *Selected Writings,* Volume 1: *Sex,* London: Gay Men's Press, 1984.

Gide, André, *The Immoralist,* translated by Dorothy Bussy, Middlesex: Penguin, 1930.

———, *Journals,* Four Volumes, translated and annotated by Justin O'Brien, London: Secker & Warburg, 1948–51.

———, *If It Die,* translated by Dorothy Bussy, Middlesex: Penguin, 1950.

———, *Oscar Wilde,* translated by Bernard Frechtman, London: William Kimber, 1951.

———, *Et nunc manet in te,* translated by Justin O'Brien, New York: Knopf, 1952.

———, *Corydon,* translated by Richard Howard, London: Gay Men's Press, 1985.

Proust, Marcel, 'La race maudite', in *Contre Sainte-Beuve,* translated by Sylvia Townsend Warner, London: Chatto & Windus, 1958.

———, *Selected Letters,* Volume 2: *1904–1909,* edited by Philip Kolb, translated by Terence Kilmartin, London: Collins, 1989.

———, *A la recherche du temps perdu,* Volume 4: *Sodome et Gomorrhe,* translated by Terence Kilmartin, London: Chatto & Windus, 1992.

———, *Selected Letters,* Volume III (1910–17), edited by P. Kolb, translated by Terence Kilmartin, London: Harper Collins, 1992.

Symonds, John Addington, *A Problem in Greek Ethics,* privately printed, London, 1871.

———, *A Problem in Modern Ethics,* privately printed, London, 1891.

———, *Sexual Inversion,* with Havelock Ellis, London: Wilson and Macmillan, 1897; reprinted New York: Arno Press, 1975.

———, *The Letters of John Addington Symonds,* edited by Herbert M. Schuller and Robert L. Peteres, Detroit: Wayne State University Press, 1969.

———, *Memoirs: The Secret Homosexual Life of a Leading Nineteenth Century Man of Letters,* edited and introduced by Phyllis Grosskurth, New York: Random House, 1984.

Secondary Texts

Abelove, Henry, 'Freud, Male Homosexuals and the Americans', in *The Lesbian and Gay Studies Reader,* edited by Barale Abelove and David Halperin, London: Routledge, 1993.

Adams, Stephen, *The Homosexual As Hero in Contemporary Fiction,* London: Vision, 1980.

Ahlstedt, Eva, *André Gide et le débat sur l'homosexualité,* Gothenburg: Acta Universitatis Gothoburgensis, 1994.

Alden, D. W., *Proust and His French Critics,* London: Lymanhouse, 1940.

Allen, Dennis W., *Sexuality in Victorian Fiction,* Oklahoma: University of Oklahoma Press, 1993.

Altman, Dennis, *Homosexual Oppression and Liberation,* London: Allen Lane, 1971.

Anonymous, *The Sins of the Cities of the Plain; or the Recollections of a Mary-Ann with short essays on Sodomy and Tribadism,* London: Privately printed, 1881.

———, *Teleny* [1884], San Francisco: Gay Sunshine Press, 1984.

Aron, Jean-Paul, and Roger Kempf, 'Triumphs and Tribulations of the Homosexual Discourse', in G. Stambolian and

E. Marks (eds), *Homosexualities and French Literature: Cultural Contexts/Critical Texts,* Ithaca: Cornell University Press, 1979

Barreca, Regina, *Desire and Imagination: Classic Essays in Sexuality,* New York: Meridian/Penguin USA, 1995.

Bartlett, Neil, *Who Was That Man? A Present For Mr. Oscar Wilde,* London: Serpent's Tail, 1989.

Bataille, Georges, *Visions of Excess: Selected Writings 1927–1939,* translated by A. Stoekl, C. R. Lovitt, and D. M Leslie Jr., University of Minnesota Press, Minneapolis, 1985.

Beach, Frank, 'Comments on the Second Dialogue in Corydon', appendix in André Gide, *Corydon,* New York: Octagon Books, 1977.

Benjamin, Jessica, *The Bonds of Love: Psychoanalysis, Feminism and the Problem of Domination,* Virago, 1990.

Berger, M., B. Wallis and S. Watson (eds), *Constructing Masculinity,* London: Routledge, 1995.

Bersani, Leo, *Homos,* Harvard University Press, 1995.

——, *The Culture of Redemption,* Harvard University Press, 1990.

Birkin, L., *Consuming Desire: Sexual Science and the Emergence of a Culture of Abundance 1871–1914,* Ithaca: Cornell University Press, 1988.

Bleys, Rudi C., *The Geography of Perversion: Male-to-male Sexual Behaviour outside the West and the Ethnographic Imagination 1750–1918,* London: Cassell, 1997.

Blumenfeld, Warren J., *Homophobia: How We All Pay the Price,* Boston: Beacon Press, 1992.

Boswell, John, *Christianity, Social Tolerance and Homosexuality: Gay People in Western Europe from the Beginning of the Christian Era to the Fourteenth Century,* Chicago: University of Chicago Press, 1980.

Bray, Alan, *Homosexuality in Renaissance Britain,* London: Gay Men's Press, 1982.

Bristow, Joseph, 'Homophobia/Misogyny: Sexual Fears, Sexual Definitions', in Simon Shepard and Mick Wallis (eds), *Com-*

ing on Strong: Gay Politics and Culture, London: Unwin Hyman, 1989.

——, *Sexual Sameness: Textual Difference in Lesbian and Gay Writing,* London: Routldge, 1992.

——, and Angela Wilson, *Activating Theory,* London: Lawrence and Wishart, 1993.

——, *Effeminate England: Homoerotic Writing After 1885,* London: Open University Press, 1995.

——, *Sexuality,* London: Routledge, 1997.

Brown, Carolyn, 'Figuring the Vampire: Death, Desire and the Image', in S. Golding (ed.), *The Eight Technologies of Otherness,* London: Routledge, 1997.

Brown, T. (ed.), *Edward Carpenter and Late Victorian Radicalism,* London: Cass, 1990.

Bullough, Vern L., *Science in the Bedroom,* New York: Basic Books, 1994.

——, and B. Bullough, *Sin, Sickness and Sanity: A History of Sexual Attitudes,* New York: New American Library, 1977.

Burton, Richard, 'Terminal Essay', in *The Thousand Nights and a Night* (1885), New York: Heritage Press, 1962.

Butler, Judith, *Gender Trouble: Feminism and the Subversion of Identity,* London: Routledge, 1990.

——, 'Imitation and Gender Subordination' in D. Fuss (ed.), *Inside/Out: Lesbian Theories, Gay Theories,* London: Routledge, 1991.

——, *Bodies That Matter: On the Discursive Limits of 'Sex",* London: Routledge, 1993.

——, *Excitable Speech: A Politics of the Performative,* London: Routledge, 1997.

Butters, Ronald R., John M. Clum, and Michael Moon, *Displacing Homophobia: Gay Male Perspectives in Literature and Culture,* Durham: Duke University Press, 1989.

Cawadias, C. P., *Hermaphroditos: The Human Intersex,* London: Heinemann, 1946.

Clephane, Irene, *Towards Sexual Freedom,* London: The Bodley Head, 1935.

Comstock, Gary David, *Violence Against Lesbians and Gay Men*, New York: Columbia University Press, 1991.

Compagnon, Antoine, *Proust: Between Two Centuries*, translated by Richard E. Goodkin, New York: Columbia University Press, 1992.

Copley, Anthony, *Sexual Moralities in France 1780–1980*, London: Routledge, 1989.

Corbin, Alain, 'Backstage', in Michelle Perrot (ed.), *A History of Private Life*, Volume 4: *From the Fires of Revolution to the Great War*, translated by Arthur Goldhammer, Cambridge MA: Belknap Press of Harvard University Press, 1990.

D'Arch Smith, Timothy, *Love in Earnest: Some Notes on the Lives and Writings of English 'Uranian' Poets 1889–1930*, London: Routledge & Kegan Paul, 1970.

Dannecker, Martin, *Theories of Homosexuality*, London: Gay Men's Press, 1981.

Davenport-Hines, Richard, *Sex, Death and Punishment: Attitudes to Sex and Sexuality in Britain Since the Renaissance*, London: Collins, 1990.

Davis, Steve, *Born That Way? The Biological Basis of Homosexuality*, Channel Four pamphlet, 1992.

Delavenay, Emile, *D. H. Lawrence and Edward Carpenter: A Study in Edwardian Transition*, London: Heinneman, 1971.

Delay, Jean, *The Youth of André Gide*, translated by June Guichamaud, Chicago: University of Chicago Press, 1963.

Deleuze, Gilles, and Félix Guattari, *Anti-Oedipus: Capitalism and Schizophrenia* [1972], translated by Robert Hurley, Mark Seem and Helen R. Lane, University of Minnesota Press, 1983.

Derrida, Jacques, *Positions*, translated by Alan Bass, London: Athlone, 1981.

Dollimore, Jonathan, *Sexual Dissidence: Augustine to Wilde, Freud to Foucault*, Oxford University Press, 1991.

Duberman, Martin, *Cures: A Gay Man's Odyssey*, New York: Plue, 1991.

Dumouchet, Paul (ed.), *Violence and Truth: On the Work of René Girard*, London: Athlone Press, 1987.

Eagleton, Terry, *Literary Theory: An Introduction,* Oxford: Basil Blackwell, 1983.

Edelman, Lee, *Homographesis,* London: Routledge, 1994.

——, 'Seeing Things: Representation, the Scene of Surveillance, and the Spectacle of Gay Male Sex', in D. Fuss, (ed.), *Inside/Out: Lesbian Theories, Gay Theories,* London: Routledge, 1991.

Ellis, Havelock, *Studies in the Psychology of Sex: Sexual Inversion,* London: Wilson & Macmillan, 1897.

——, 'A Note on the Bedborough Trial', Watford University Press [1898], privately printed, D.C. McMurtie, 1925.

——, *Psychology of Sex,* London: Heinneman, 1933.

Ellman, Richard, *Oscar Wilde,* London: Hamish Hamilton, 1987.

Fletcher, John, 'Forster's Self-Erasure: Maurice and the Scene of Masculine Love', in Joseph Bristow (ed.), *Sexual Sameness,* London: Routledge, 1992.

Foucault, Michel, *The Birth of the Clinic: An Archaeology of Medical Perception,* translated by A.M. Sheridan Smith, London: Routledge, 1973.

——, *The Order of Things: An Archaeology of the Human Sciences,* translated by A.M. Sheridan Smith, New York: Vintage Books, 1973.

——, *The Archaeology of Knowledge,* translated by A.M. Sheridan Smith, New York: Harper Colophon, 1976.

——, *The History of Sexuality,* Volume 1: *An Introduction,* translated by Robert Hurley, Harmondsworth: Penguin, 1979.

—— (ed.), *Herculine Barbin, Being the Recently Discovered Memoirs of a Nineteenth Century Hermaphrodite,* translated by Richar McDougall, Harvester Press, 1980.

——, *The History of Sexuality,* Volume 2: *The Use of Pleasure,* translated by R. Hurley, Harmondsworth: Penguin, 1985.

——, *The History of Sexuality,* Volume 3: *The Care of the Self,* translated by R. Hurley, Harmondsworth: Penguin, 1986.

——, *Foucault Live: Interviews 1966–84,* New York: Semiotext(e), 1989.

Fout, J. C. (ed.), *Forbidden History: The State, Society and the Regulation of Sexuality in Modern Europe,* Chicago: University of Chicago Press, 1992.

Freud, Sigmund, *Standard Edition of the Complete Works,* Volume II, translated by James Strachey, London: Hogarth Press, 1964.

——, 'Three Essays on Sexuality', in *The Pelican Freud Library,* Volume VII, edited by Angela Richards, Harmondsworth: Penguin, 1986.

Fryer, Jonathan, *André and Oscar: Gide, Wilde and the Gay Art of Living,* London: Constable, 1997.

Fuss, Diana, *Essentially Speaking: Feminism, Nature and Difference,* London: Routledge, 1989.

Gallop, Jane, *Feminism and Psychoanalysis: The Daughter's Seduction,* London: Macmillan, 1982.

——, *Thinking Through the Body,* New York: Columbia University Press, 1988.

Garber, Marjorie, *Vested Interests: Cross-Dressing and Cultural Anxiety,* Harmondsworth: Penguin, 1992.

Gardiner, M., *The Wolf-Man and Sigmund Freud,* Harmondsworth: Penguin, 1973.

Geraci, Joseph (ed.), *Dares To Speak: Historical and Contemporary Perspectives on Boy-Love,* London: Gay Men's Press, 1997.

Girard, René (ed.), *Proust: A Collection of Critical Essays,* New York: Prentice-Hall, 1962.

Goldberg, Jonathan, *Reclaiming Sodom,* London: Routledge, 1994.

Golding, Sue (ed.), *The Eight Technologies of Otherness,* London: Routledge, 1997.

Green, F. C., *The Mind of Proust: A Detailed Interpretation of 'A la recherché du temps perdu',* Cambridge: Cambridge University Press, 1949.

Greenberg, David F., *The Construction of Homosexuality,* University of Chicago Press, 1988.

Greer, Germaine, *Sex and Destiny: The Politics of Human Fertility,* London: Picador, 1984.

Grosskurth, Phyllis, *John Addington Symonds: A Biography*, London: Longmans, Green & Co Ltd, 1964.
——, *Havelock Ellis: A Biography*, Toronto: McCellan and Stewart, 1980.
——, *Introduction to The Memoirs of John Addington Symonds*, New York: Random House, 1984.
Hallam, Paul, *The Book of Sodom*, London: Verso, 1993.
Halley, Janet E. 'The Politics of the Closet: Towards Equal Protection for Gay, Lesbian and Bisexual Identity', in S. Goldberg, *Reclaiming Sodom*, London: Routledge, 1994.
Halperin, David M., *One Hundred Years of Homosexuality*, London: Routledge, 1990.
——, 'Is There a History of Sexuality?', in *The Lesbian and Gay Studies Reader*, Routledge, 1993.
——, *Saint Foucault: Towards a Gay Hagiography*, Oxford University Press, 1995.
Hamer, Dean, and Peter Copeland, *The Science of Desire: The Search for the Gay Gene and the Biology of Behaviour*, New York: Simon & Schuster, 1994.
Haver, William, *The Body of This Death: Historicity and Sociality in the Time of AIDS*, Stanford University Press, 1996.
——, 'Queer Research: Or How to Practice Invention to the Brink of Intelligibility', in S. Golding (ed.), *The Eight Technologies of Otherness*, London: Routledge, 1997.
Hayman, Ronald, *Proust: A Biography*, London: Heinemann, 1990.
Hekma, Gert, 'A History of Sexology', in J. Bremmer (ed.), *From Sappho to De Sade: Moments in the History of Sexuality*, London: Routledge, 1989.
——, 'Homosexual Behaviour in the Nineteenth-Century Dutch Army', in J. C. Fout (ed.), *Forbidden History: The State, Society and the Regulation of Sexuality in Modern Europe*, Chicago: University of Chicago Press, 1992.
——, '"A Female Soul in a Male Body": Sexual Inversion as Gender Inversion in Nineteenth Century Sexology', in Gilbert Herdt (ed.), *Third Sex Third Gender: Beyond Sexual*

Dimorphism in Culture and History, New York: Zone Books, 1994.

Higgins, Patrick, *A Queer Reader*, London: Fourth Estate, 1993.

Hindus, Milton, *The Proustian Vision*, New York: Columbia University Press, 1954.

Hirschfeld, Magnus, 'The Homosexual As an Intersex', in C. Berg and A.M. Krich (eds), *Homosexuality: A Subjective and Objective Investigation*, London: Allen & Unwin, 1958.

Hocquenghem, Guy, *Homosexual Desire*, translated by D. Dangor, Durham: Duke University Press, 1993.

Hodson, Leighton (ed.), *Marcel Proust and the Critical Heritage*, London: Routledge, 1990.

Howard, Richard, 'From Exoticism to Homosexuality', in G. Stambolian and E. Marks (eds), *Homosexualities and French Literature: Cultural Contexts/Critical Texts*, Ithaca: Cornell University Press, 1979.

Hutter, Jorg, 'The Social Construction of Homosexuals in the Nineteenth Century: The Shift from Sin to the Influence of Medicine on Criminalizing Sodomy in Germany', in John P. DeCecco and John P. Elia (eds), *If You Seduce A Straight Person Can You Make Them Gay?*, New York: Harrington Park Press, 1993.

Hyde, Montgomery H., *The Other Love: An Historical and Contemporary Survey of Homosexuality in Britain*, London: Heinneman, 1970.

Jordanova, Ludmilla (ed.), *Languages of Nature: Critical Essays on Science and Literature*, London: Free Association Books, 1986.

Katz, Jonathan N., The Invention of Heterosexuality, Harmondsworth: Penguin, 1995.

Kellogg, Stuart (ed.), *Literary Visions of Homosexuality*, New York: The Haworth Press, 1983.

Kennedy, Hubert, *Ulrichs: The Life and Works of Karl Heinrich Ulrichs, Pioneer of the Modern Gay Movement*, New York: Alyson Publications, 1988.

———, with Harry Oosterhuis, *Homosexuality and Male Bonding in Pre-Nazi Germany,* New York: Harrington Park Press, 1991.

Kilmartin, Terence (ed.), *Marcel Proust: An English Tribute,* London: Chatto & Windus, 1923.

Koestenbaum, Wayne, *Double Talk: The Erotics of Male Literary Collaboration,* London: Routledge, 1989.

Kopelson, Kevin, *Love's Litany: The Writing of Modern Homoerotics,* New York: Stanford University Press, 1994.

Krafft-Ebing, Richard von, *Psychopathia Sexualis,* translated by Chaddock, C. G., London: F. A. Davis, 1893.

Krala, Jay 'Male Homosexuality and Lesbianism in the Works of Proust and Gide', in L. Crew, (ed.) *The Gay Academic,* Palm Springs: ETC, 1978.

Laqueur, Thomas, *Making Sex,* Harvard University Press, 1990.

Lacan, Jacques, 'The Meaning of the Phallus', translated by Jacqueline Rose, in J. Mitchell and J. Rose (eds), *Feminine Sexuality: Jacques Lacan and the Ecole Freudienne,* London: Macmillan, 1982.

Lauritsen, John and David Thorstad, *The Early Homosexual Rights Movement,* New York: Times Change Press, 1974.

Le Vay, Simon, *The Sexual Brain,* Cambridge, MA: MIT Press, 1993.

———, *Queer Science: The Use and Abuse of Research into Homosexuality,* Cambridge, MA: MIT Press, 1996.

Lemaitre, Georges, *Four French Novelists,* Oxford: Oxford University Press, 1938.

Lewes, Kenneth, *The Psychoanalytic Theory of Male Homosexuality,* London: Quartet, 1988.

Lucey, Michael, *Gide's Bent: Sexuality, Politics, Writing,* Oxford University Press, 1995.

McNay, Lois, *Foucault: A Critical Introduction,* Cambridge: Polity Press, 1994.

Macdonnell, Diane, *Theories of Discourse: An Introduction,* Oxford: Basil Blackwell, 1986.

Marcus, Steven, *The Other Victorians,* London: Book Club Associates, 1970.

Marcuse, Herbert, *Eros and Civilisation: A Philosophical Inquiry into Freud* [1956], London: Ark, 1987.
Marmor, Judd (ed.), *Sexual Inversion*, New York: Basic Books, 1965.
Marshall, Bill, *Guy Hocquenghem: Theorising the Gay Nation*, London: Pluto Press, 1996.
Maurois, André, *The Quest for Proust*, translated by Gerard Hopkins, Harmondsworth: Penguin, 1950.
Mayne, Xavier [Edward Irenaeus Prime Stevenson], *The Intersexes: A History of Simisexualism as a Problem in Social Life*, London: privately printed, 1908.
Mendes-Leite, Rommel, and Pierre-Olivier de Busscher (eds), *Gay Studies From the French Cultures*, New York: Harrington Park Press, 1993.
Meyer, Moe (ed.), *The Politics and Poetics of Camp*, London: Routledge, 1994.
Meyers, Jeffrey, *Homosexuality and Literature 1890–1930*, London: Athlone Press, 1977.
Michel-Thiriet, Philippe, *The Book of Proust*, translated by Jan Dalley, London: Chatto & Windus, 1989.
Mieli, Mario, *Homosexuality and Liberation: Elements of a Gay Critique*, translated by David Fernbach, London: Gay Men's Press, 1980.
Millet, Kate, *Sexual Politics*, London: Abacus, 1972.
Miller, D. A., *The Novel and the Police*, Berkeley: University of California Press, 1988.
——, *Bringing Out Roland Barthes*, Berkeley: University of California Press, 1992.
——, 'Sontag's Urbanity', in Abelove, B. and Halperin, D. (eds), *The Lesbian and Gay Studies Reader*, London: Routledge, 1993.
Miller, Neil, *Out of the Past: Gay and Lesbian History from 1869 to the Present*, London: Vintage, 1995.
Milligan, Don, *Sex Life: A Critical Commentary on the History of Sexuality*, London: Pluto Press, 1993.
Mondimore, Francis Mark, *A Natural History of Homosexuality*, Baltimore: The Johns Hopkins University Press, 1996.

Money, John, *Gay, Straight and Inbetween: The Sexology of Erotic Orientation,* Oxford: Oxford University Press, 1988.

Norton, Rictor, *Mother Clap's Molly House,* London: Gay Men's Press, 1992.

Oosterhuis, Harry, 'Richard von Krafft-Ebing's "Step-Children of Nature": Psychiatry and the Making of Homosexual Identity', in Vernon A. Rosario (ed.), *Science and Homosexualities,* London: Routledge, 1997.

Owens, Craig, 'Outlaws: Gay Men in Feminism', in L. Jardine and P. Smith (eds), *Men On Feminism,* London: Methuen, 1987.

Painter, George, D., *Marcel Proust: A Biography,* revised edition, London: Pimlico, 1996.

Pascal, Mark (ed.), *Varieties of Man/Boy Love,* New York: Wallace Hamilton Press, 1992.

Perrot, M. (ed.), *A History of Private Life,* Volume IV: *From the Fires of Revolution to the Great War,* Cambridge, MA: Belknap Press of Harvard University Press, 1990.

Pollard, Patrick, *André Gide: Homosexual Moralist,* Yale University Press, 1991.

Probyn, Elspeth, 'Queer Belongings', in E. Probyn and E. Grosz (eds), *Sexy Bodies: The Strange Carnalities of Feminism,* London: Routledge, 1995

Plummer, Kenneth (ed.), *The Making of the Modern Homosexual,* London: Hutchinson, 1981.

Raffalovich, Marc, *Uranisme et unisexualite: Étude sur différentes manifestations de l'instinct sexuel,* Paris: Masson & Cie, 1896.

Reade, Brian, *Sexual Heretics: Male Homosexuality in English Literature from 1850–1900,* London: Routledge & Kegan Paul, 1970.

Rivers, J. E., *Proust and the Art of Love: The Aesthetics of Sexuality in the Life, Times and Art of Marcel Proust,* Columbia University Press, New York, 1980.

Riviere, Joan, 'Womanliness as Masquerade', in V. Burgin, J. Donald and C. Kaplan (eds), *Formations of Fantasy,* London: Methuen, 1986.

Robinson, Christopher, *Scandal in the Ink: Male and Female Homosexuality in 20th Century French Literature,* London: Cassell, 1995.

Rosario, Vernon A., *Science and Homosexualities,* London: Routledge, 1997.

Rose, J. and J. Mitchell, *Feminine Sexuality: Jacques Lacan and the École Freudienne,* London: Macmillan, 1982.

Ross, Michael W., *Homosexuality, Masculinity and Femininity,* New York: Harrington Park Press, 1983.

Rousseau, G. S., *Perilous Enlightenment,* Manchester: Manchester University Press, 1991.

Ruse, Michael, *Homosexuality: A Philosophical Inquiry,* Oxford: Basil Blackwell, 1988.

Sedgwick, Eve Kosofsky, *Between Men: English Literature and Male Homosocial Desire,* New York: Columbia University Press, 1985.

——, *Epistemology of the Closet,* Berkeley: University of California Press, 1990.

——, *Tendencies,* London: Routledge, 1994.

Segal, Lynn, *Slow Motion: Changing Masculinities, Changing Men,* London: Virago, 1990.

——, *Straight Sex: The Politics of Pleasure,* London: Virago, 1994.

Seiden, Melvin, 'Proust's Marcel and Saint-Loup: Inversion Reconsidered', in B.J. Bucknall (ed.), *Critical Essays on Marcel Proust,* London: G.K. Hall & Co, 1987.

Shattuck, Roger, *Proust,* London: Fontana/Collins, 1974.

Shepherd, Simon, and Mick Wallis (eds), *Coming On Strong: Gay Politics and Culture,* London: Unwin Hyman, 1989.

Showalter, Elaine, *Sexual Anarchy: Gender and Culture at the Fin de Siècle,* London: Virago, 1990.

Silverman, Kaja, *Male Subjectivity at the Margins,* London: Routledge, 1992.

Silverstolpe, Frederic, 'Benkert Was Not a Doctor: On the Non-Medical Origins of the Homosexual Category in the Nineteenth Century', unpublished conference paper from

Homosexuality, Which Homosexuality? Conference, Free University of Amsterdam, 1987.

Sinfield, Alan, *The Wilde Century: Effeminacy, Oscar Wilde and the Queer Moment,* London: Cassell, 1994.

Smith, Anna-Marie, *New Right Discourse on Race and Sexuality,* Cambridge: Cambridge University Press, 1994.

Sontag, Susan, 'Notes on Camp', in *The Susan Sontag Reader,* edited by Elizabeth Hardwick, Harmondsworth: Penguin, 1982.

Spencer, Colin, *Homosexuality: A History,* London: Fourth Estate, 1994.

Starkie, Enid, *Gide,* Cambridge: Bowes & Bowes, 1953.

Steakley, James D., *The Homosexual Emancipation Movement in Germany,* New York: Arno Press, 1975.

Stein, Edward (ed.), *Forms of Desire: Sexual Orientation and the Social Constructionist Controversy,* London: Routledge, 1992.

Steiner, George, 'Eros and Idiom', in *On Difficulty and Other Essays,* Oxford: Oxford University Press, 1978.

Straus, Bernard, *The Maladies of Marcel Proust,* New York: Homes and Meier, 1980.

Sullivan, Andrew, *Virtually Normal: An Argument About Homosexuality,* London: Picador, 1996.

Tatchell, Peter, *We Don't Want to March Straight: Masculinity, Gays and the Military,* London: Cassell, 1995.

Tedeschi, P. (ed.), *Selected Letters of André Gide and Dorothy Bussy,* Oxford: Oxford University Press, 1983.

Theweleit, Klaus, *Male Fantasies*, Two Volumes, Cambridge: Polity Press, 1987–9.

Thiele, Beverley, 'Coming-of-Age: Edward Carpenter on Sex & Reproduction', in T. Brown (ed.), *Edward Carpenter and Late Victorian Radicalism,* London: Cass, 1990.

Thody, Philip, *Marcel Proust,* London: MacMillan, 1987.

Trumbach, Randolph, 'Gender and the Homosexual Role in Modern Western Culture: The Eighteenth and Nineteenth Centuries Compared', in *Homosexuality Which Homosexuality?,* London: Gay Men's Press, 1989.

Tsuzuki, Chuschichi, *Edward Carpenter 1844–1929: Prophet of Human Fellowship,* Cambridge University Press, 1990.

Van der Meer, Theo, 'Sodomy and the pursuit of the Third Sex in the Early Modern Period', in G. Herdt (ed.), *Third Sex, Third Gender: Beyond Sexual Dimorphism in Culture and History,* New York: Zone Books, 1994.

Van Leer, David, *The Queening of America: Gay Culture in Straight Society,* London: Routledge, 1995.

Warner, Michael, *Fear of a Queer Planet: Queer Politics and Social Theory,* Minneapolis: University of Minnesota Press, 1993.

Watney, Simon, *Policing Desire: Pornography, AIDS and the Media,* London: Methuen, 1987.

———, 'Gene Wars', in M. Berger et al. (eds), *Constructing Masculinity,* London: Routledge, 1995.

Weeks, Jeffrey, *Coming Out: Homosexual Politics in Britain From the Nineteenth Century to the Present,* London: Quartet, 1977.

———, 'Discourse, Desire and Sexual Deviance: Some Problems in a History of Homosexuality', in K. Plummer (ed.), T*he Making of the Modern Homosexual,* London, Hutchinson, 1981.

———, *Sex, Politics and Society: The Regulation of Sexuality since 1800,* London: Longman, 1981.

———, *Sexuality and Its Discontents*, London: Routledge Kegan Paul, 1985.

———, *Against Nature: Essays on History, Sexuality and Identity,* London: Rivers Oram Press, 1991.

———, *Invented Moralities: Sexual Values in an Age of Uncertainty,* Cambridge: Polity Press, 1995.

———, with Sheila Rowbotham, *Socialism and the New Life: The Personal and Sexual Politics of Edward Carpenter and Havelock Ellis,* London: Pluto Press, 1977.

Whisman, Vera, *Queer By Choice: Lesbians, Gay Men and the Politics of Identity,* London: Routledge, 1996.

Wolff, Charlotte,*Magnus Hirschfeld: A Portrait of a Pioneer in Sexology,* London: Quartet, 1986.

Young, Ian, *The Stonewall Experiment,* London: Cassell, 1995.

Journals

Apter, Emily S., 'Homotexual Counter-codes: André Gide and the Poetics of Engagement', *Michigan Romance Studies* 6, 1986.

Bersani, Leo, '"The Culture of Redemption": Marcel Proust and Melanie Klein', *Critical Inquiry* 12.2, 1986.

———, 'Is the Rectum a Grave?', *October* 43, 1987.

Birke, Lynda, 'Zipping up the genes: Putting biological theories back in the closet', *Perversions* 1, Winter 1994.

Bristow, Joseph, 'Being Gay: Politics, Identity, Pleasure', *New Formations* 2.9, Winter 1989.

Butler, Judith, 'Critically Queer', *GLQ: A Journal of Lesbian & Gay Studies* 1.1, 1993.

De Lauretis, 'Queer Theory: Lesbian and Gay Sexualities: An Introduction', *Differences: A Journal of Feminist Cultural Studies* 3.2, 1991.

Dollimore, Jonathan, 'Homophobia and Sexual Difference', *Sexual Difference,* Oxford Literary Review, 1986.

Duggan, Lisa, 'The Discipline Problem: Queer Theory Meets Lesbian and Gay History', *GLQ: A Journal of Lesbian and Gay Studies* 2.3, 1995.

Fuss, Diana, 'Pink Freud', *GLQ: A Journal of Lesbian and Gay Studies* 2.1–2, 1995.

Golding, Sue, 'Sexual Manners', *Public* 3, 1990.

———, 'The Excess: An Added Remark on Sex, Rubber, Ethics, and Other Impurities', *New Formations* 19: 'Perversity', Spring 1993.

Hekma, Gert, 'The Homosexual, the Queen and models of Gay History', *Perversions* 3, Autumn 1994.

Julian, Isaac, and Savage, Jon (eds), *Critical Quarterly* 36.1: Critically Queer Issue, Spring 1994.

Kader, Cheryl, and Piontek, Thomas (eds), *Discourse: Journal of Theoretical Studies in Media and Culture* 15.1: Lesbian & Gay Studies Issue, Fall 1992.

Kingman, Sharon, 'Nature Not Nurture?' *The Independent on Sunday*, 4 October 1992.

Le Vay, Simon, 'A Difference in Hypothalamic Structure Between Heterosexual and Homosexual Men', *Science* 253, 1991: 1034–7.

Lynch, Michael, 'Here is Adhesiveness: From Friendship to Homosexuality', *Victorian Studies* 29, 1985.

Mager, Don, 'Gay Theories of Gender Role Deviance', *SubStance* 46, 1985.

Moran, Leslie, 'Buggery and the Tradition of the Law', *New Formations* 19: 'Perversity' Issue, Spring 1993.

O'Brien, Justin, 'Albertine the Ambiguous: Notes on Proust's Transposition of the Sexes', PMLA 64, 1949.

Pollard, Patrick, 'André Gide, Corydon and this Adversaries', *European Gay Review* 4, 1988.

Rosenberg, Marjorie, 'Inventing the Homosexual', *Commentary* 84, December 1987.

Schmidt, Gunter, 'Magnus Hirschfeld (1868–1935), *European Gay Review* 5, 1989.

Trumbach, R., 'London's Sodomites: Homosexual Behaviour and Western Culture in the Eighteenth Century', *Journal of Social History* 11, 1977.

Watney, Simon, 'The Homosexual Body: Resources and a note on theory', *Public* 3, 1990.

Weeks, Jeffrey, 'Sins and Diseases: Some Notes on Homosexuality in the Nineteenth Century', *History Workshop* 1, 1977.

www.ingramcontent.com/pod-product-compliance
Lightning Source LLC
Chambersburg PA
CBHW031500160426
43195CB00010BB/1044